2,50

How to Write Articles
for Profit and PR

How to Write Articles for Profit and PR

MEL LEWIS

**KOGAN
PAGE**

Acknowledgements

Thanks are due to the MI Group, notably Operations Director Peter George and Marketing Manager Stephen Auty; PNA Managing Director Bill Gibbs; Cristina Stuart, author of *Effective Speaking* and Managing Director of Speakeasy. Closer to home, Beverley Jayne Shipp, SEN, nursed me through many a writer's tantrum and hangover during the preparation of this book, and helped me see some of my own points more clearly.

First published in Great Britain in 1989 by
Kogan Page Limited, 120 Pentonville Road,
London N1 9JN.

British Library Cataloguing in Publication Data
Lewis, Mel
  How to write articles for profit and PR
  1. Creative writing – Manuals
  I. Title
  808'.042

  ISBN 1-85091-840-6
  ISBN 1-85091-841-4 Pbk

Printed and bound in Great Britain by
Biddles Limited, Guildford

For Zelda, forever

Contents

Preface

I take issue with a lot of pundits on writing. I don't believe everyone can earn 'big money' as a writer or even ever be able to turn out a good, readable 500-word feature at the drop of a Pritt Stick. For some it will always be hard going, and most of the time they won't even wish to bother. Why should this be so?

I don't know. But I know this. First, that motivation – sheer wanting to write and being prepared to go about it in a methodical way – counts for more than any innate flair.

Curiously, a 'gift of the gab' may not translate easily into fluent writing skill. By the time we mark someone out as gab-gifted, they've been talking for some time and it has become second nature. Professional writing technique comes relatively late in life. The silver-tongue syndrome suggests a light touch, gregariousness. Writing is a head-down, 'academic' activity, and a lonely one. It takes study, practice, sweat and a mean streak. You have to be jealous of what other writers can achieve and determined to get there, too.

Perhaps 'enthusiasm' is a better word than motivation here. Make writing work and it will give you a good life. What other occupation lets you sit on your butt all day, in your own home, and earn a more than comfortable living? Writing can be fun. But the best fun is when the cheques start tumbling through the letterbox.

1
The Market

We called this book *How to Write Articles for Profit and PR* because it opens up, probably for the first time in one volume, the wide range of activities that a professional writer can tackle. And it shows, moreover, how anyone in virtually any business can use the techniques it reveals to improve their business or their image through effective – and cost-effective – PR.

There is meat here for many industry professionals – marketing, advertising, communications, personnel executives – not to mention those already working in PR, who are told, frequently and accurately, that their press releases are binned ninety times out of a hundred.

Many will no doubt use this book to handle their publicity and PR work themselves, and cut corners on cost and time – and good luck to them. Those who continue to use outside PR agencies and consultants will still be ahead of the game. Studying *How to Write Articles for Profit and PR*, they will understand what works in writing and why, and as a result will be better equipped to monitor and cost the PR work they commission and pay for.

Most intriguingly, this book explores the twilight zone between 'straight' journalism and commercial writing. Many writers on so-called independent newspapers and magazines keep other irons in the fire as fee-paid publicists, writing press releases, brochure material, sponsored 'advertorial' (promotional writing masquerading as editorial copy), ghosting speeches, and so on.

Unlike Members of Parliament who must declare their outside interests, journalists are largely on their mettle – which is why *Private Eye* magazine, which lifts the lid on the extra-curricular activities of journalists, makes such interesting reading!

Far from being an exposé of commercial work, then, this book

11

is an endorsement of it. The fact is, PR work is usually better paid, more readily available (there are more people in more businesses than there are editors to work for), at least as interesting and better appreciated by those who commission and pay for it.

The greatest joy of PR is that it puts you in the company of *business people*.

Editors may be great campaigning journalists, design geniuses, outstanding communicators. But I never met one who was naturally or voluntarily businesslike in his or her dealings with me. Being a good editor isn't about being good at business; indeed, editors don't normally handle their own money. They merely manage a budget on behalf of a board of sober-suited individuals.

Since an early rule of business is that you try to deal only with principals, be advised that in this respect editors simply don't qualify.

The truth, in the words of the late great copywriter Lou de Swart, is that 'You are your own best client.' Not many writers know this, and fewer still act on it. One way to be your own client is to make (or otherwise acquire) your own product, handling your own marketing and doing your own deals. As far as writing is concerned, this quintessentially businesslike activity is known as syndication. It is dealt with at length in Chapter 7, page 115.

Isn't freelance writing a saturated market, with too many operators chasing too few assignments? Following cutbacks on papers and healthy redundancy payments to encourage people to stay out of regular employment, more journalists than ever are relying on their 'mercenary' writing abilities to make a living.

By and large, though, ex-staffers have little enough idea how to operate a writing business profitably and efficiently, which is where this book will help.

For those who aren't angling to be well-paid, professional writers, there is another compelling reason to read on. In many industries and professions, being published in one's own field brings considerable kudos. Becoming known as an expert commentator or an entertaining pundit is a high-profile activity for an executive. And a high profile is no bad thing to have when heads are being hunted.

2
Ideas and Where to Get Them

Brainstorming for ideas and inspiration

Professional writers don't wait for ideas to hit them. They woo inspiration. They discover how to 'get in the mood', to be receptive to ideas; then they just jot them down and store them up.

People who write for a living have more ideas than they know what to do with, so the problem becomes: 'Which is the best idea, which should I proceed with first, which will sell the easiest, which will involve the least amount of original research before I pen the letter which clinches the assignment?' And so on.

Ideas are ten a penny. Fleshing them out is the real craft. And wanting to, being sufficiently motivated even to bother, is the greater challenge. Eighteenth-century critic Samuel Johnson declared that only a blockhead ever wrote, except for money. His words are as true today, at least as far as non-fiction is concerned.

To earn good money you need material to work with – loads of ideas from which to pick and choose. Find what encourages the creative flow in you, then OD on it. I prefer showers to baths, but for some folk, a long hot bath encourages the Eureka! effect that Archimedes made famous.

Sometimes the problem is clearing the mind of mundane anxieties, such as where the money is coming from to pay the phone bill or book the next holiday. Jogging helps. I don't think when I run; I go into a kind of trance – naturally produced opiate derivatives seep into the brain after 20 minutes of energetic activity, I read somewhere. This may account for the dream-like condition. Who cares? It works. So does fast motorcycling, though not too fast or incautious, or you may find your brain literally emptied – all over the road. The point with the latter activity is that concentration is of necessity absolute if one is to stay alive.

Sometimes an alcoholic drink or two or three helps to spin the cogs. What you are aiming for – it suddenly occurs to me – is the 'elation effect', however induced. A few pints in a pub at lunchtime also work for me. I sit there pen in hand, pad open, rarely blank for long. The skill is to control the pace of drinking, so you can crystallise thoughts for long enough to get something worthwhile down before passing out.

It also helps to have some reward on hand, such as a favourite newspaper, book, or a piece of research from a project that's going well. Once you switch to the second activity, useful thoughts from the earlier brainstorming session seem to percolate through.

Some writers have a relationship with their writing instruments. Hemingway used to sharpen 15 pencils before he felt comfortable enough to launch into a writing session – standing up at a lectern, for preference. I have some fads and have abandoned a number of others. I've tried all the fancy pens – Mont Blanc, Waterman, the fat, black cigar-size ones with the fancy gold bands on, the Chinese-lacquered Parkers and the antique Conway Stewart. My current favourite is a black Sheaffer bought in a sale for half its £60 normal retail price. All fountain pens leak, by the way, whatever the ads say.

As well as your main writing tool, you also need a 'highlighter', though preferably not an actual one, which is too watery. The idea is that you can ring and underline and join ideas from one end of the page to the other in an indelible way. Any red or vivid colour pen will do; the best, however, is the nylon-tipped Papermate.

Hardware apart, an old writer's wrinkle will help. Get something down on paper. Write a word, a sentence, any old rubbish, destroy the blankness of the page. Your whole body is a machine; and that includes the brain. Machines run smoother, faster when they're used and warm and have reached a point where the impetus neatly overcomes all the forces acting to slow them down, and the bare minimum of energy is needed to keep the wheels turning. All this applies with a vengeance to writing, and equally to the 'foreplay' of good, profitable writing activity – producing a flow of interesting, worthwhile ideas.

What can I write about?

'Nothing ever happens to me' or 'Nothing interesting ever happens to me' is a common cry from a non-writer who likes the idea of being a writer and wants me to deliver a crash course, on the spot, on how it's all done, even though they will never do anything about it except carry on being a passive reader. But you're different. You are motivated enough to be reading this book, which in itself will make you a more interesting person, and put you on the road to being a writer who has a sporting chance of getting into print.

Since I cannot talk you through your own experiences and show you how fascinating they actually might be to an editor, consider this. 'I' pieces, articles where the writer relates something that happened to him or her are relatively few on the printed page. The exceptions are with regular columnists whose brief is to run amusingly through 'their week'; gifted occasional contributors who can turn anything into an amusing or intriguing anecdote; or where the first-person piece is by a celebrity.

Most of the time the reader is concerned about a very different 'I', one much closer to home; the one who lives inside his or her own body, in fact. Appeal to self-interest and you will always have a ready audience. All you need do is twist your 'I' piece round until it becomes a much more saleable 'you' piece. Let's look at some specifics.

I was going through a busy but bad patch as a writer. Why bad? I was doing a lot of work, but having a hard time getting paid by a number of clients. I needed to discover what was the best way to turn a slow payer into a prompt cheque-signer. How should you approach someone who owes you money without falling out with them, yet still get down to brass tacks? How do you sue someone and win? And so on.

Slow payment was a blight of those severely straightened times, so I knew other people were suffering similarly. I could have written a piece about how tough things were for me. But I didn't. I wrote a book called *How to Collect Money That Is Owed to You* (McGraw-Hill, 1981). The book has sold close on 6000 copies, has been translated into Spanish and chosen by *The Economist* for inclusion in their *Best Business Books* guide. I've also lectured on the topic and written articles around what I now take to be an ace title for a follow-up book: *How to Ensure Prompt Payment of All Your Business Bills*, the point being that you are trying to avoid collection problems through an awesome billing technique and positive stance. Read the book when it comes out!

It is said that the purpose of all writing is to persuade, inform or entertain. One thing is sure: the biggest paying market revolves around writing that informs.

Combine self-interest with information and you have a winning formula for the rest of your writing days. What do we mean by self-interest? What do people really worry about?

Well, we have a number of basic drives, such as hunger and thirst, the latter being by far the more urgent quest. Did you know that a person will die after a week to ten days with no water, but can live up to a month with drink but no food? A camel can remain its grumpy self for three weeks without a drink, and then regain its usual bad temper after a 30-gallon drink. Can you see articles in this theme? Hands up those who can't.

Other basic human needs? Sleep, elimination of body wastes, breathing, sweating, salivating. When shelter, food and physical well-being are assured we have other interests, loosely described as 'play activities'. I can't believe the Lascaux cavemen found much time for cave painting while they were under siege by giant tigers or wondering where the next roast meal was coming from. Can you? And when every personal need is satisfied, thoughts turn to the greatest leisure activity of all . . . sex.

Of course, these needs – lusts, almost – apply almost as well to any creature. Human drives, based on these primitive urges, are more complex. Women exhibit maternal behaviour; men are traditionally preoccupied with self-assertion; we are all to one degree or another gregarious and would like to be more so in most cases. We are also acquisitive, obsessed with possessions.

At school the English and French masters – and the class – talked nonchalantly, knowingly, about 'the human condition', how it pervades the best literature, and so on. Until I was about 40 'the human condition', as far as I was concerned, might as well have been a problem a hairdresser could cure. What was meant, of course, was the single powerful secret that truly separates man from other animals – knowledge of death.

These, then, are some of the themes that run through writing that works, writing that gets sold and read. Write on food, shelter, clothing, safety, health, sex, nurturing relationships, self-esteem, money. Money relates to prestige, fame. Food can mean entertaining. Combine the two and you get an article title such as: 'Even a Pauper Can Eat Like a King.'

Sex isn't just 'the act'; it's also love, marriage, a happy home, children. Health extends to exercise, fitness, sport, winning. Learn how to spike your writing with these heady ingredients, involve your readers personally, and you will always find editors willing to spend time studying your ideas and offer you commissions.

Ideas blowing in the wind

'Everything comes to him who waits', they tried to brainwash me, as an impatient child. Later, as the most callow adult, you discover it just ain't true. It isn't even true of people standing at a bus stop – just look at their blank, justifiably pessimistic faces! Nor does it apply to the pursuit of ideas worth writing about. No, I much prefer the old Persian proverb, 'Luck is infatuated with the efficient.'

Ideas need to be stalked, targeted, captured, categorised, husbanded. They are all around, but only for those with eyes that are trained to see. People say to me, 'Where do you get your ideas from?' Or they sigh, 'Nothing like that ever happens to me.'

I turned the following ideas into articles which were published in national newspapers and magazines. The experiences that sparked them were casual enough. The cheques that followed provided the real excitement.

How one idea leads to another

The stuff of feature ideas is all around us. Learning how to spark an idea at will, often right there on the phone, talking to an editor, or in his office, is a skill that comes with insight and practice. Yet this

17

ability can mean the difference between the occasional commission and a regular flow of work – and an editor who eventually picks the phone up and calls you with assignments, rather than you forever chasing him. The way you get good at 'spouting' ideas, as with other activities, is to practise in private; in this case in your head and on paper.

In 1974, as a freelancer, I approached the editor of *Money Mail*, a section of the *Daily Mail* which had started to appear every Wednesday. *Money Mail* presented financial topics in a lighter, brighter way than the traditionally heavy, figure-laden City pages.

Everyone is interested in money, the *Mail* reasoned. All we need do is serve it up in the right way. Look at it another way. Not everyone goes for that dry-looking carrot cake. But turn it into a layer cake, add a thick, sweet, creamy topping and call it passion cake, and the potential market multiplies wildly.

Money Mail, of course, was not an entirely altruistic concept. The paper was (still is) able to use the extra page area around *Money Mail* features to sell advertising space to financial institutions and others, keen to penetrate the consumer and family money market.

The art editor specified bold, feature-page style headings, big pictures, big spreads, the opened-out centre two pages often being treated as one large design area. And, of course, more popular themes were permitted than the usual fusty diet of stocks and shares, takeover bids, director appointments, and so on.

I did what every writing textbook counsels. I approached the editor with a subject I knew: antiques. You don't have to do this. But it makes sense, as writing on a familiar topic is easy writing. And when the editor asks questions or probes alternative or subsidiary angles, the information is there, at your fingertips.

My first piece (I think – the writing relationship lasted ten years) was about the then 'new' phenomenon of one-day antique fairs. Actually, the fairs weren't new, only the duration and the low cost of hiring a pitch and erecting a folding table for your goods. The paper called the story: 'The Dignified Way to Make a Profit.' I began:

CASH FROM ANTIQUES, an old story, has been given a

Cinderella twist. Collectors now have the opportunity to become dealers for a day.

If you're a collector with an oversize collection it means you can sell off 'doubles' of pieces you've fallen out of love with – and you don't have to set up shop to do it.

The story went down well with the *Mail* and in other areas. As a journalist, nothing gives you a profile quite as high as when your work appears in a popular daily paper. It raised my standing in the antiques business, and the fairs organiser I interviewed in the article repaid me with free pitches at her future events. This enabled me to learn insider dealing tricks first hand. And when her business boomed and she started her own little newsletter I became a paid contributor to that.

My immediate concern was to build on this *Money Mail* 'in'. This I did throughout 1974 and 1975. In early 1976 I was searching for a fresh angle on the usual press pontification that precedes the spring Budget. At a friend's house one day, I happened to be discussing the economy with her two intelligent children, aged 15 and 13. I was surprised to discover that the kids, who were at boarding school, had vehement, if informed, right-wing opinions. Nothing wrong with that, just that their words would not have been out of place coming from the mouth of some crusty old retired colonel in Chipping Something. I knew I had my article. I would suggest a piece where kids commented on the economy.

The article, a big-paying centre-page spread, appeared under the banner: 'If You Think Managing the Country's Economy Should Be Child's Play.' The headline read: 'Out of the Mouths of Babes and Budding Chancellors.'

The article kicked off:

Who can make Britain Great again? Our chosen politicians with their teams of economic advisers and batteries of computers . . . not on current form, it seems.

Perhaps they're using the wrong tools. Or trying too hard. Adults are like that. 'All the king's horses and all the king's men couldn't put Humpty together again.'

But a solitary child might have – with a tube of glue.

Perhaps a fresh and naive approach would help with our monetary difficulties, too.

Another time I was a bemused bystander to a fairly heated 'discussion' between this same friend and her offspring. Pocket money was the problem. The kids reckoned they weren't getting enough of it. My article appeared in *Money Mail* entitled: 'Are Your Children Due For a Rise?'

Of course, I used different children interviewees, though one or two might have been friends or relatives of the original two media starlets.

The trick, as with any type of business marketing move, is to find what people want and give them more of it. I'd cultivated this skill years earlier as a teenager earning Saturday pocket money selling clothes in menswear shops in East London. Generally, the managers bought a batch of ties, shirts, socks, and so on, in a predictable range of colours – red, blue, green, perhaps grey. Everyone knew that in the end you would probably shift more of the blue than any other hue, since that is (or certainly was) the taste of the western world, and this was reflected in the way the managers stocked up.

You would never know that any particular customer would favour blue but you did know what colours he was wearing that day; you could see his hair and eye coloration; and it took no great genius to suggest more of the same and be rewarded, often, with an easy sale.

When it comes to your literary outpourings, the same goes for commissioning editors.

You've heard it said: 'There's nothing new under the sun.' It's true. The adage applies mercilessly to feature ideas. Of course, Bernard Shaw could not have written about space shuttles; they didn't exist in his day. But exploration themes did. The trick, if you are not serving up news, is to find a fresh angle, a slant which will intrigue readers. Ahead of that, of course, you must first tease and tantalise an editor into accepting your work.

Try some 'Janusian thinking' even if it isn't January

Janus is the January god of the Romans. He had two heads to enable him to look backwards to the dark days of winter as well as forwards to the 'dapple-dewed' days of spring. Janusian thinking can be a powerful spur to creativity. All it means is that you tack two odd ideas together and see what happens. Since you are trying to go into 'free fall' with your imagination, the odder these ideas are – to start with – the better.

Suppose Shakespeare is one of your pet subjects. You know that there are already thousands of books written on the Bard, and an even greater stack of articles. Still you hanker after adding to the body of literature. 'Shakespeare and . . . ' (add your own name) has quite a nice ring to it, you reckon! In spite of the lack of originality of the ambition, there are two things that count in your favour. First, no matter how much has been said about the world's most famous dramatist, the last word has not been written – nor ever will it. Second, people obviously have a voracious appetite for material on WS or why would all those other authors have bothered and their work been published?

So what can you say that's new? I have a book called *Shakespeare and Music*. Slightly more exotic might be Shakespeare and Fashion. A wider reading public might warm to Shakespeare and Food. Shakespeare and Sex would also find a ready audience; as, too, Shakespeare and Homosexuality, since the controversy over the mysterious, possibly male, lover of the sonnets will no doubt continue to rage long after we two are gone and forgotten. However, as these possibilities fairly trilled from my fingertips, you can take it they have been done to death and you would need to work hard to sell such well-worked commodities.

How about this: Shakespeare and the Shylock Syndrome? I don't know what a 'Shylock Syndrome' is, but I could make a damn good job of inventing one! I also know that readers (and that means editors who filter, approve and pay for your writing) seem to like these quasi-scientific titles.

It's true. Look at Parkinson's Law (briefly stated, work expands

21

to fill the time available to do it in); the Peter Principle (everybody in a business hierarchy tends to rise to his or her level of incompetence); the Po-Po Principle (managers who believe talent and drive will ensure their advancement, who foolishly renounce office politics and get Pissed On and Passed Over – the book is a survival guide) – all big selling business books.

Let's try another theme. Marilyn Monroe.

Monroe and Morality
Monroe and Other Screen Immortals
Monroe and the Mafia

As the assassination of President Kennedy has been linked with the Mafia, and Marilyn Monroe has been romantically linked with the Kennedy clan, I'm using literary licence and going for the jackpot. Something else you might have noticed: alliteration – or possibly assonance, the pleasant rhyming effect achieved through repeating consonant or vowel sounds – is also likely to win you editorial approval, provided it isn't forced. Here's one that I like the sound of: Masters and Johnson and the New Morality. Sex sells. So might an absence of it, in literary form, in our AIDS-conscious climate.

Money for nothing – and your cheques for free

Plundering local papers for marketable articles is easy, once you develop a writer's way of looking at news and information. In *Motor Cycle News* I spied an item about a chap who had started a motor bike museum in the yard of an antiques market in Essex. Biking is a hobby, but writing a column on antique fairs and markets for *Antique & Collectors Fayre* is one of my steady, fee-paying assignments. A phone call or two gave me an unusual story and helped to fill column inches with minimum effort.

Not every publication is a gold-mine. But my copy of *Diss Mercury and Advertiser* dated 18 November 1988 certainly was.

You've heard about the feats of motor bike riders Evel Knievel and Eddie Kidd, the youngster who rode his bike clean over umpteen buses to earn a place in the *Guinness Book of Records* that has yet to be challenged. The *Mercury* ran a piece on 'Motor biker Ben Taylor' who 'cleared a 60ft river [the Waveney] on a scrambling machine'.

Since I'm interested in the subject I might suggest a piece to *Motor Cycle News,* or one of the many biker magazines, on stunt riding. They would be interested to know that Ben did his motorised leap, with 6ft to spare, aboard a lowly 250cc Honda scrambler bike. He was travelling at 60mph when he left the ramp specially designed by buddy Adrian Bird. You can just picture the sketch which might accompany such an article, which would explain how to calculate trajectories, take-off velocity, and so on.

The 'why' of it all could furnish another feature. Ben did the jump with his mother's curlers attached to the crown of his crash helmet. Why? 'So that people would be able to see me in the water if I sank!' He was aiming to raise money for the West Suffolk Hospital, Bury St Edmunds, as a thank you to staff who had nursed his broken bones, sustained in numerous scrambling accidents.

Some time back I did a piece on a despatch rider who worked for PNA, a company which specialises in the distribution of press releases and media information generally. I was writing a newsletter, ads and mailshots to promote the services PNA offers. The biker had beautiful auburn hair down to his shoulders. In fact, from behind he was a dead ringer for Rula Lenska. As a dare, and to raise money for a cancer charity, Mark had his hair cropped so short he needed a new crash helmet.

The story made a good pair of pictures for the PNA newsletter, and I also sent them to *BAIE News,* the paper put out by a professional association to which I subscribe, the British Association of Industrial Editors. The editor was looking for eye-catching pictures submitted by members and mine was the first to be used in the series.

It occurs to me that there is a piece to be written on the nice things that bikers, a much maligned species, thanks to a handful of speed freaks, do. Despatch riding itself is worth a longer treatment. It's a dangerous, lonely profession, riding against the clock in dense city traffic. Yet I hear of £500 a week take-home pay, and the only qualification is the ability to ride a motor cycle and make sense of an intercom unit strapped to your chest that sounds like Donald Duck talking under water.

A London cab driver once described his occupation as 'the last stand of the independent man'. 'Talk to any cabbie and you'll see he's tried all sorts of businesses, and they all flopped. This [cabbing] is all that's left,' he explained. Was there a similar tale of woe among despatch riders? Or, more likely, was this the only kind of free-wheeling, high-pay work these youngsters could hope to find, given the employment situation?

I press on with the *Mercury*. Under the heading 'Julie Finds Herself Warming to Life on the Kibbutz', I read about 23-year-old Julie Thurlow, 'one of four people chosen in a Young Farmers' national exchange scheme to study the agricultural system in Israel.' Judging from the photograph and the name, I'd say Julie was a non-Jew. Would her 'outsider' story, with its practical slant, find a home in a paper like the *Jewish Chronicle*?

On page 12 police are warning about 'bogus salesmen'. Home owners in the Attleborough area are warned to be 'on their guard against door-to-door salesmen claiming to be deaf'. As a foot-in-the-door ploy this is hard to beat. What if the salesman turns out to be a villain?

Editors love this type of public service story. It locks on to every reader's anxiety about his or her home, possessions, loved ones. I see this making part of a larger article warning against all the tricks con men and pushy tradespeople use to break down barriers and get inside homes. The police will no doubt provide good quotes and case histories. This story is so strong that, with a little more research and some hair-raising real-life stories, a national paper might take it.

Considering the *Diss Mercury and Advertiser* is a freesheet, I consider it to have been damn good value for no money!

3
The Raw Material of Writing

Gold that's delivered every day

Top comedian Benny Hill says his perfect day off involves buying all the daily papers and reading through the lot at leisure. He says newspapers are a gold-mine of ideas for comic sketches. The same goes for ideas for articles. He's right on the other count, too: savouring the news is a luxury. I gave it up years ago. Now I don't have papers delivered or even see anything, except the *London Evening Standard*, on a daily basis.

Instead, I have my local newsagent stockpile the following: *Daily Mail* and *Daily Express* every Wednesday, just for the 'pop' money sections; *Campaign* for inside information on advertising campaigns and industry personalities; *UK Press Gazette*, to keep up with the coming and goings of Fleet Street; *Antique Dealer and Collector's Guide*, an essential guide to upmarket activities of antique dealers and antique fairs organisers, my clients among them.

Money Marketing, PR Week, Antiques Trade Gazette and *Contributor's Bulletin* are delivered through the post. Just about the only thing I insist on buying on publication day each week, and read cover to cover, is *Motor Cycle News*. But that's pure escapism, and more often than not, I read *MCN* as a relaxing reward for having completed some strategic, cash-culling activity.

As for the other papers and magazines, I never actually 'read' them at all. I scan and 'gut' them, which means looking through, marking interesting items with a red felt-tip, then snipping them out, ready for filing at a later date. I trust you spotted my deliberate mistake . . .

Every cutting is also *dated* and *attributed*. I know a lot of people don't do this, or do it but don't appreciate the importance of the exercise and leave off this vital information. So often, PR handouts contain glowing write-ups on clients from the cuttings file, *minus* the name of the paper from which the clipping came, and usually sans date for good measure. It creates a credibility gap that works against the purpose of PR and is easily avoided.

Filing made easy

Filing is a tedious, time-consuming activity, but an essential one. The trick is not to let it get out of hand, by which I mean, don't be too obsessional about ordering your notes for articles, self-memos, cuttings, and so on, at too early a stage.

The main aim of a filing system is that you don't lose things. Sorting through material that you know is there somewhere is as nothing to having to find stuff that has gone missing. If everything connected with a particular topic or department is in one place, even if that place is a box, you are winning.

Part of my own filing system includes a series of 17 × 14 × 10in plastic Curver boxes. I had six or seven when I was handling a lot of regular journalistic work. One was labelled 'Parents', into which I threw prompts for my erstwhile legal and financial column. Another box was entitled 'Antiques', and served a similar function for my *Antique & Collectors Fayre* and *Antique Dealer and Collector's Guide* monthly spots. There were also 'Miscellaneous', 'Ideas' and 'Correspondence' Curvers.

The boxes look like nothing on earth and won't impress visitors or your partner; plus they take up valuable floor space (though they do stack); but they *work* (they will also take a foolscap-size A-Z concertina file, with a section for every letter), and that's what matters.

Anything that encourages speedy, fairly accurate filing is worth having. If your filing system obliges you to type neat sticky labels, remove your derrière from your writing chair and go walkabout in search of envelope folders and the appropriate hanging Twinlock files, it's probably pulling you away from that more urgent activity which is called *writing*.

The Curver system is a vertical filing system, since the bits of paper go on top of other bits of paper. Filing cabinets, those filing systems on wheels (I have a Media-Stor version of the latter) and files that hang in cupboards, rather like suits in a wardrobe, are all horizontal filing systems. Horizontal systems have a secondary role in filing, in my view and in my office. Here is where I put articles and associated research material, propositioning and commissioning letters, and so on, *after* the articles have been completed.

I puzzled for some years over why, in some respects, horizontal systems have the edge over the 'pile it high' system of filing; why they hold more, in other words. The secret was revealed to me after I bought a Ryman trolley file equipped with a dozen or so plastic trays and a useful work top. The trays had sides about two inches deep and would therefore take a pile of papers about 1½in high in practice. Each tray had about 2½in of air above it, separating it from its tray neighbours, above and below. A horizontal filing system, where you can sloosh the files along a rail to insert new material, makes do with just one 2½in gap for all the files. The wedge of air is movable, so to speak, with the result that the same amount of filing space takes a far greater number of files.

But no system, to my mind, takes adequate account of the fact that most articles generate a combination of simple pieces of paper, scraps with notes on, press releases, and also fairly bulky reports and booklets. The latter tumble out of normal files, given time and the workings of Murphy's Law. A solution is available, however, in the shape of the Collecta A4 filing system.

Imagine a classic box file (in the Eastlight mould) but made out of plastic, not cardboard, and with cutaway sides. These files stand on their short ends and are about the width of two London telephone directories (another use for Collecta, by the way). I generally put all my pieces of paper into A4 size Ryman Pentos transparent PVC folders ('open two sides, stepped and thumbcut', as the packaging has it). Bulkier items can be stood upright, alongside the bits of paper, which are more inclined to 'stand to attention' in their PVC jackets. Pentos files consume shelf space like nobody's business, and are about a fiver a pair, so not cheap, but they are well worth the investment in order and ease of handling.

Another use I've found for Collecta is to hold 'runs' of magazines, such as the square-bound *Antique Dealer and Collector's Guide*, or the floppier issues of the American publications, *Writer* and *Writer's Digest* – provided they're stacked tight enough so they don't collapse at the base of the spine.

The greatest filing area, of course, is your floor, which offers one of the best arguments for having a large study, and is worth bearing in mind if you work from home and the room you are being allocated is, according to tradition, the second smallest room in the home. Nick Anning, former lecturer in Russian at London University and a *Sunday Times* writer, showed me how to work on the floor, as it were.

He worked from the flat we shared in Kennington; I was an IPC staffer at the time and only modestly involved in freelance. Nick showed me how each project, with its own assortment of books and notes, commanded two square feet of floor space. It was worth relinquishing the best den in the flat for this piece of information alone.

How to preserve your cuttings

Filing cuttings is a nuisance, on a number of counts. Newsprint, for obvious reasons, is rubbish quality and quickly goes brown and crumbles if exposed to light, heat or damp. Photocopies have a longer life, so if you can find a cheap route to photocopying your cuttings, take it and throw away the originals. Alternatively, store them in damp-proof zip folders, the ones with transparent sides and bright coloured plastic zippers on top.

How to proposition a PRO

The prolific, successful writer wants to be 'assaulted' by information. But he doesn't want to waste time with material, however interesting, if it doesn't trigger writing ideas or offer research nuggets. So though I am forever filling in coupons and contacting sources offering free information, I have also become ruthless at junking material sometimes stillborn in its envelope. It's a rare skill and one worth cultivating. Just don't make any mistakes!

One of the little-appreciated sources of free information is PR people. PROs, Public Relations Officers, are paid to assemble tantalising press releases, news stories and newsletters which give their paying clients a high profile, and present the goods or services the client sells in a favourable light. That's usually the aim. The wolf may wear sheep's clothing, as you will see in Chapter 6, and also a lot of the time the wolf turns out to be a pretty toothless beast, who fails miserably to achieve coverage for clients. Because the law of averages (at least) tends to work in their favour, even with indifferent work and poor targeting, PROs tend to shift a lot of paper, since this is likely to improve their chances of landing a story in one medium or the other.

It will often pay you to get on their mailing lists for free information. Much of it will be useless; some will provide no-cost on-the-job training in how not to write a press release; and occasionally you will pick up a tip, an angle and also some free photographs, often a vital ingredient in a selling story (more about photographs on page 75).

Curiously, asking for these freebies, which are scattered across the media like confetti, immediately raises suspicions – probably that you work for some rival PR agency out to steal the account and are trying to assemble a portfolio of their indifferent material in order to rubbish it and steal the business. It's nuts, but an accurate portrayal of life in a paranoid profession. As a result, you will need to sell yourself to a PR agency as a prolific journalist with good contacts in areas that matter to the agency.

However naff PR operatives might be, they do know where they would, *at best*, like their work/clients' names to appear. So target your sales letter intelligently. Here's an example designed to succeed with the PR outfit of a motor manufacturer.

Dear . . .

A SIGNIFICANT MINORITY AUDIENCE FOR INFORMATION ON YOUR ESTATE VEHICLES

As you can see from this letterhead and the enclosed cuttings, I write on antiques and collecting. Antique dealers are demanding motorists. They frequently cover hundreds of miles for a single transaction, and those who exhibit at fairs – my special responsibility – may spend the greater part of their working lives on the road.

By far the most common vehicle found in the car parks at such events is the Volvo. Yet you know, and I know, that there are other estates – probably . . . . 's [name client] estates among them – worthy of equal consideration.

With the editor's permission naming no names: I don't want any particular editor approached over my head; or he could get the week-long test drives that I intend to arrange and enjoy at a later date! I will be surveying the estate and large hatch market on a regular basis.

Therefore, I would appreciate being placed on your regular mailing list for news on suitable . . . . [name client] estate models.

Appreciatively yours,

Sincerely

MEL LEWIS

Two important points will dramatically improve your chances of winning friends and influencing people among the PR fraternity. First, write only on suitably impressive headed paper which under-lines the message that you are a busy, much-read writer – more on professional presentation in Chapter 5.

To save time, when mailing a number of agencies with the same begging message, you can simply take a stack of your letterheads to the local instant print shop. The actual letter to be reproduced on the letterheads is perfectly typed on *plain* white paper. You've made sure that the layout of the letter on the white piece of paper fits comfortably, stylishly, on a piece of your letterhead by laying the plain sheet on top and checking where your address etc inter-feres with available print area.

The print shop will then overprint the typed sheet on to the headed paper. If you have a tractor feed or sheet-feeder facility on your own printer, obviously you can handle repeat printing at an even lower cost.

The second point is much more important. If you want to cultivate a friend in public relations, send him cuttings which you have originated that feature his client's name. This obviously does you good, because it tells the PRO that helping you was a smart move. It also helps your PR contact, because he can then show the client what a clever chap he is, what great Press contacts he has engineered, and so on. This is an obvious point, but one that journalists can easily overlook.

The more Fleet Street wise among you might remark that the client/PR agency will have hired a press clippings agency (such as Durrants or Romeike & Curtice) to keep track of reports as they appear. Not necessarily so. Clients are forever cutting corners on costs, to the chagrin of PR operatives who, unless they pay the clipping company themselves, may never know the full extent of their successes – or failures.

The bottom line is: take all your freebies, then pay your dues. It's the best way to get even more help from PROs at a rock bottom price – nothing.

4
Professional Writing Techniques That All Writers Must Learn and Remember

How to 'energise' your writing

I just did just that. I 'energised' my title by using the words 'how to'. 'How to' is one of those magic openers. It tells the reader that he is going to learn something. As a writer, all you need do then is lock on to something that the reader wants to know, the more passionately the better, and add that to the equation. 'How to' works as hard for you in the text as it does in a title.

How to Win Friends and Influence People, published in the 1930s, sold millions of copies for author Dale Carnegie and publishers Simon & Schuster on the strength of a mail order ad that bore the same headline as the book title.

The ad closed with an irresistible guarantee – 'send no money'. And fabulous credentials: 'This book has been published for only a short time. Yet it is now outselling any other book – fiction or non-fiction – in America! The presses are now running continuously to turn out 5000 copies daily.' Another energising fillip.

It's one thing to say a book is hugely successful, something else to quantify it in a forceful and believable fashion. If you consider that a business book is likely to have a first printing of around 3000 copies, and will be lucky to go into a second printing inside a year, if at all, Carnegie's book was selling like ice packs in Hell.

Every topic under the sun is a candidate for the 'how to' treatment. I've picked eight books at random off my shelves: *How to Undo a Maiden; How to Start and Manage Your Own Business; How to Buy (Almost Anything) Secondhand; How to Make Effective Business*

Presentations; How to Become a Bestselling Author; How to Buy Fine Wines; How to Write Comedy; How Managers Make Things Happen. There must be something appealing about the promise contained in the words 'how to'. One of my more esoteric finds is a book called *How to Write 'How To' Books*!

Never be afraid of being old fashioned and using the words 'how to'. There have been many attempts to ring the changes on these words. Some writers view the words 'how to' as what writing 'clinician' Elmer Wheeler called 'shiny in the pants' words, but they're wrong. Nothing prompts that 'tell me more' response quite as effectively as 'how to', though people are right to *try* to be different.

Elliot, the publishers, brought out a successful series of books under the banner heading, Elliot Right Way Books – The Right Way To . . . pass your motor cycle driving test, buy antiques, sell a house, and so on. Sometimes the 'how to' is left off, as with Alastair Crompton's paperback, *Do Your Own Advertising*. It could easily have been *How to Do Your Own Advertising*. I can think of one good reason for missing off words. It's easier to get the title on the spine.

Such short cuts are meant to cut the cackle. They overlook the fact that people are creatures of habit, and that 'how to' is so much a part of our language and culture that it triggers response in much the same way as 'Once upon a time . . . ' does to a child. It tells the child, and the child in all of us, that we are now going to hear, or read, a story. Once upon a time there was a way to write that made it hard for a reader to stop reading . . .

When I talk about energising writing, I mean giving it impetus, sparky phrases, using techniques that power the reader on to read the rest of your copy. So much of writing, especially academic writing, has, to my mind, an enormous conceit – or misplaced confidence. The writer appears to take it for granted that his work will get read as of right.

The reality, as my copywriting guru Lou de Swart pointed out, is that most people are busy people, open to all kinds of stimulation and distraction, so that to a writer they are moving targets and must be caught and captured using a variety of techniques whose one aim is to 'keep 'em reading'.

How to write titles that crash an editor's apathy barrier

A title – or a headline – has one main function. To intrigue the reader and keep him reading. You can't normally tell a story in a handful of words. But you can grab interest and tease the reader into persevering with your message.

'Message' is a better word than 'story'. Because headlines – also called 'heads', 'headings' and 'titles' – apply to a lot more than articles. And as a writer in search of fee-paying assignments you are involved in other types of headlines, as well as journalistic headlines, as we'll see.

Headlines sit on advertisements, precede the spiel in sales letters, appear on book jackets, and so on. Never doubt the power of a good headline. 'The headline can make or break your advertisement' said Lou de Swart. David Ogilvy, one of advertising's legendary figures, founder of Ogilvy & Mather, one of the world's most successful agencies, and himself an ace copywriter, remarked that 'On the average, five times as many people read the headlines as read the body copy'. It follows, says Ogilvy, that unless your headline sells your product, you have wasted most of your money.

Both these experts cut their teeth on onyx – in the hard school of mail order, where the key to success is constant testing. Lou de Swart said a headline must do two things: define your market and promise benefits. One of the greatest headlines of all time appeared on an ad for men's shoes that featured a concealed platform to make the wearer look taller. The headline doesn't mention 'shoes'. But by golly, the copywriter who wrote 'GIRLS LOVE TALL MEN' knew his market!

What has copywriting got to do with writing for newspapers, journals and books? Consider this: 1947, an otherwise inauspicious year, saw the publication of a book entitled *The Way to Write*, probably the finest writing textbook ever published. In spite of the implication that this is *the* one, the only, the best way to write, as opposed to merely 'a' way to write, the title is curiously limp given the writerly perceptions of authors Rudolf Flesch and A H Lass.

In the 1960s the book was republished in paperback as *A New Guide to Better Writing*. Now do you see how words can wilt on you or work for you?

Almost everything benefits from a good heading

Headings give you a break, a breathing space in which to collect your thoughts, knowing you can return to a convenient place. But their main function is to tease the reader into going on. For this reason, the professional writer uses them to good effect in many places.

The best laid-out magazine and newspaper articles use neat headings called cross-heads, usually only two or three words long, to break up the text and relieve the eye. The most sophisticated commercial writing, which I take to be top-class American copywriting, goes further. Here, the cross-heads actually highlight the key or selling points in telegraph form.

Research reveals that people read inattentively and most simply won't read any particular advertisement unless the headline grabs them by the throat. The smart copywriter reasons that, having gone for the jugular with his heading, he can still get his selling story across by highlighting the benefits of the product in the cross-heads. That way, even if a reader simply scans the ad, he'll still get the message.

I like to use this technique even at manuscript stage. It pays to assume people *don't* want to read your stuff – or at least they haven't much time to spend on it. So with a manuscript of more than 1000 words (four to five sides of A4 paper, double-spaced), I insert headings/cross-heads, perhaps one every two pages, so that the editor doesn't feel intimidated by a sea of copy, and can get my drift at a glance.

He also knows, of course, that I've had editorial office training, and being a professional he'll respond more favourably to a fellow professional. Such is the way of the world. But you can hack it too, now, by following my lead.

Headings that sell articles

Editors are like any other punter: they need to be coaxed, intrigued, teased into reading and that includes the sales letters you send containing ideas for articles. With a couple of small provisos. Editors are as busy as anyone in any business. But they are even more jaded when it comes to reading. Your headings need to hit hard and quick in the right spot, so don't waste words. The best opening sentences have five to eight words, no more. Why not apply the same rule to headings? See what happens under this small discipline. Overall, though, be guided by the copywriter's rule of thumb: a heading is as long as it needs to be to get your message across.

Something more about editors. They all seem to have what Hemingway called his 'built-in shit detector'. Let me explain. I was once asked by a *Daily Mail* editor to dig up the dirt on driving schools. I spent some time on it but found no fresh slant on the well-known abuses. But I put all these down in what I thought was a lively letter, that could almost have served as an article in itself. The editor was furious. 'There's nothing fresh in this. You've wasted five minutes of my time.' I would have done better to have come clean and shelved the idea until I turned up a worthwhile piece of grit.

A corollary is that you should not 'flam it up', as they say in local newspaper offices – give a story an importance it doesn't deserve.

A while back I sent out a query letter based on an item I'd read in *World's Fair*, the trade paper for fair-ground people. It was about an expert in the education of fair-ground children. As a new father, I was taken with the business of schooling, and I thought the added ingredient of teaching itinerant children might make a thought-provoking piece.

Aware that this was no centre-page feature, I was at pains to dream up a heading which would attract without promising the earth. I settled on a quote taken verbatim from the *World's Fair* cutting, a photocopy of which I enclosed. It read: 'Bob Frequently Lectures on Fair-ground Children's Education.'

Another time I had a much more potent story. My dentist told me about a strange and disturbing discovery reported in a dental journal. The gist was that fluoride, meant to make teeth 'decay proof', may actually encourage serious and deep-seated decay. The query letter was headed: 'Has Fluoride Failed?'

For the outline of an article that looked at photography from an unusual angle (the practice and experience of people who regularly take pictures, but don't consider themselves to be photographers – folk such as estate agents, auctioneers, antique dealers, and so on), I chose the title: 'Secrets of the Snapping Professionals'.

One useful trick is to pick up on famous or popular titles. In the wake of the bestseller *The One Minute Manager*, came *The 59 Second Employee*. (I always had a hankering to write a spoof called *The One Minute Lover*!) Other titles have also had their day, spawning a host of article title lookalikes. How many of these have you seen in a bastardised form: *The Spy Who Came in From The Cold, Lateral Thinking, Chips with Everything, Saturday Night and Sunday Morning*?

I capitalised on the currency of *Everything You Always Wanted to Know About Sex, But Were Always Too Afraid to Ask* with an idea for a series of loony articles, offered under the banner: 'Everything You Never Wanted To Know About . . . But Would Be Intrigued To Discover Anyway'.

We return to these examples in Chapter 7; the titles are truly part of a complete sales technique for marketing article ideas and should be viewed in context.

How do you get good at headings?

How do you get good at anything? The time-honoured effective way is to study, practise, put into practice. When it comes to writing, many people, career journalists among them, neglect step one with a vengeance. Very few writers seem to have read much on writing – even ex-college people whom you would have thought would be sold on book learning.

They seem unaware of, and sometimes positively indifferent to, the Fort Knox of information that is flimsily locked up in books. Of course, a similar nonchalance is found in many occupations. 'If people are paying good money for my skills,' the professional reasons, 'surely I know enough and don't have to ''go back to school''.' Well, you now know better.

The point about books is that they are a short cut to wisdom, the next best thing to sitting at the feet of a master. Treat them, therefore, with the profound disrespect in which you should hold all experts, soi-disant or otherwise. 'Disrespect'? Sure. For all sorts of reasons.

Books are written by people, and people have axes to grind, angles to sell. I remember, always with a grin, the leaflet on mail order published in America over 20 years ago. It cost just one dollar and was fabulous value for money. The author was at pains to explain why he was giving away so much wisdom for just one dollar. His argument ran that by 'educating' his potential writing rivals he would be forced by the competition to become an even better writer himself.

I believe the true marketing pitch for the booklet is accounted for by the late Jack Cohen's pricing policy for Tesco, the food chain: 'Pile 'em high and sell 'em cheap.'

So don't give people, authors included, the benefit of the doubt – check 'em out. And the best way to do this is to cross-reference. To read loads of books/chapters on the same aspect of writing – 'how to get started' is, in itself, an aspect of writing. If all the writers are saying roughly the same thing, it's probably right.

Incidentally, this technique overcomes one of the bugbears of book learning, namely that we don't take much in at first glance. But instead of having constantly to re-read, something I find tedious, this way you get to digest the same thing, but it always has a different flavour.

How you can limber up as a wordsmith

It's all very well my telling you how I do something like writing headings; I've spent years going through the journalistic mill. How do *you* do it? What counts as practice for a committed and money-motivated 'outsider'?

I have a number of suggestions. Use these exercises to limber up. But be aware that they are as a punch-bag to a boxer: tremendous for building writerly muscle tone, developing reflexes, and so on; but never, quite, the real thing.

The ideas that follow are mainly practice for headings, but in fact they'll help your writing in every department. The aim is to improve on existing 'telegraph' style writing. What I mean is that in daily life we encounter a lot of writing that is meant to be brief, instructive, straightforward, and so on, but in fact fails more or less miserably. Things such as road signs, instructions, and the like. I once wrote a piece for the *Daily Mail* on the rules you find in children's games. Would you believe that one sentence, supposed to be explaining how to play a board game to a child, contained 90 words!

The essence of a good heading is that it is short, sweet, snappy, hits hard and fast, and so on. You would have thought these same principles ought to be guiding the people who write 'life and death' instructions for passengers travelling on British Rail. You would have thought wrong. Consider this gem culled from the corridor of a train:

> Tools and appliances
> are kept in the guard's compartment
> for use in emergency.

Is 'tools' the most important word here? Picture a passenger, nursing his fractured collar bone, covered in crud and peppered with shattered glass, crawling through the upside down corridor of a derailed train.

Maybe 'emergency' is the more urgent word. Perhaps we could slap a big 'EMERGENCY' label on the notice and then start with 'Tools'. Or start off with 'Emergency tools'. In either case, at a stroke we've lost 'for use in'. There's also a certain long-winded casualness about 'are kept in the ... ' that is, how shall I say, inappropriate in these dire circumstances.

As for 'appliances', I don't rightly know what they might be. Do you? I remember Zanussi, the fridge and cooker maker's 'Appliance of Science' advertising campaign. 'Appliances' sounds a bit vague and lavatorial, especially in a sign attached to the outer wall of the WC, as it was on this train. I think we could make do with 'tools' and leave the 'appliances' to the imagination. This gives us:

Emergency tools
in guard's compartment.

And then we could (should?) go stark staring mad and tell travellers where the guard's compartment might be. There might just be some disorientation following a head-on crash. (I'm old enough to remember when guards travelled about in the last car on a train, in a funny little carriage, with a balcony at each end and a stove-pipe with a dunce's hat on snaking up somewhere from the roof; so they presumably kept warm and brewed a lot of tea. But where do our guards live *today*?)

This kind of word game is easy and fun. Played by the right people, it might even help save a few lives. Here's another game anyone can play. The synonym game.

You know what a second-hand car is. But if you follow the H R Owen dealership ads in the *Sunday Times* you'll have seen that you can invest in such a thing as a 'pre-owned' Rolls-Royce. Now believe me, it's easier to send up this kind of thing than to better it – assuming, of course, that 'second-hand' needs improving. What can you come up with?

nearly new
as new
like new
newish
barely used
lightly used
carefully used

If circumstances warrant it, consider this tack:

low mileage
nominal mileage
minimal mileage

I don't like any of these better than I like 'pre-owned'. A 'pre-owned' glass is the kind of glass you send back in a restaurant because you can see the previous 'owner's' lipstick on it. It needs something zappy... How about

recent Rolls-Royces?

Ah, now we're getting somewhere. 'Recent', in this case, is what writers sometimes term a weasel word. The upshot is that you can get away with anything in writing, or life, if you can find the right form of words. Better yet is the line currently being used offering 'born again BMWs'.

Here's another useful brain-whirler for wordsmiths. How many sales can you have? I've seen 'end of season sale', 'clearance sale', 'stocktaking sale', 'closing down sale', 'mid-season sale', 'everything-must-go sale', 'sale of the century', 'silly sale', and so on.

The trouble is, people don't trust salesmen or saleswomen, and they don't trust sales either. The trick is to come up with a sale that sounds genuine. 'Genuine reductions' sounds everything but; it's the feeling you get when the salesman says, 'Trust me.' The hairs prickle at the back of the neck.

Let's dig a little. What do people really want from a sale? Do they want the goods for nothing? I suggest not. People are so suspicious, they would probably run a mile if shops started giving goods away. What they most want is the retail margin knocked out of the transaction. People hate the idea of a retailer making what they take to be an easy profit.

This suggests:

wholesale prices
warehouse clearance
goods at cost

One of the franchised car dealers runs a sale offering cars at cost plus 4 per cent. We know they're having their pips squeaked at this price, but somehow it still feels like I'm giving someone pocket money, and I don't like it.

Read all about it!

Here's a writing exercise that's closer to home. For the purpose of this game you are the sub-editor who has to compose the billboard teaser that will sell the latest edition of the evening newspaper. This is the scrawled, raucous headline 'poster' that goes under the trellis-topped sandwich board by the feet of the newspaper vendor.

Before we start, a couple of observations. When I left my first-ever job as a sub-editor on *She*, after a brief period of freelancing as a sub on the *TV Times*, I went the time-honoured route and learned the ropes on a provincial paper – well, the London equivalent of it. I became a sub on the *Stratford Express* in East London.

In the normal way, you would be a reporter first, and then come in from the cold, get your feet under a desk and learn all the desk skills of the sub-editor – editing copy, demolishing libels, designing pages, creating headlines, intros, captions, working with printers, cutting copy 'on the stone', where the 'hot metal' type lay in inky black rows in the forme.

Soon enough I was entrusted with my own 'slip edition', a version of the newspaper which included several pages of interest local to one of our newer circulation areas. I became virtually the chief sub of the *Barking & Dagenham Express*. Each week, on the eve of publication, Trevor Bond, the editor, came to me for local story lines, the copy that would (we hoped) ensure strong local sales when the headlines appeared on the billboards where the newspapers were on sale.

I remember these few words as being hard work, and Trevor having little difficulty in improving on my efforts.

I also remember something else from the far-from-dim past. When London boasted several evening papers the vendor used to yell something that sounded like 'Starrnewseestandard!', referring, of course, to the *Star, Evening News* and *Evening Standard*, followed by a news preview, such as 'War declared!' or similar, to encourage newspaper sales.

The *Standard* always had better billboard writers than the *Evening News*. Perhaps the *News* died the death from this affliction alone; we'll never know. What is obvious, though, is that the billboard writer's job is an important one. See how we get on.

The fictional lead story you're working with is this: a woman has been raped in a London supermarket and has killed her assailant with a fruit knife.

The billboards are always written in capital letters, and there are usually no more than four or five 'decks' or rows of writing. As if that wasn't enough, there is also a practical limit to the 'character count' across any row – you probably won't have room for more than nine or ten letters, with the space between words counted as one space.

This type of exercise is similar to the day-to-day work of the sub-editor, who is constantly having to fit headlines into constricted spaces, but more exquisitely demanding in addition. With our billboard there is virtually no room for literary or grammatical manoeuvre. Besides which, there is often a stricture on which angle starts the copy. If you are trying to pick up local sales, you have to ring the right bell with the first word.

I see at least seven possible ways to start this story-in-a-nutshell; starting with the London, woman, rape, rapist, knife, death or foodstore angles. Let's start with 'London' and see what happens.

LONDON
RAPE
WOMAN
KILLS
ATTACKER

You could substitute 'VICTIM' for 'WOMAN'. But 'WOMAN' is more emotive. I'm not sure whether it pays to say the man's dead, or whether there is more tension gained from saying he was stabbed or knifed. Remember, prompting an 'Is he dead?' curiosity in the passer-by may result in the purchase of a newspaper, the sole object of this writing exercise.

WOMAN
KNIFES
ATTACKER
AFTER
FOODSTORE
RAPE

I'm a bit worried about 'AFTER', but 'FOLLOWING' would be too cumbersome. The 'FOODSTORE' bit appeals to my sense of the bizarre. Only pedants will complain that it wasn't the foodstore that was raped...

RAPE
VICTIM

STABS
FOODSTORE
ATTACKER

I quite like the word 'SLAYS', instead of 'STABS', but maybe it's a mite too transatlantic.

RAPIST
KNIFED IN
'DEATH WISH'
REVENGE
KILLING

There, I've got in a cinematic allusion – and underlined the message that this was *revenge*.

KNIFED
RAPIST
DIES. 'WHY
I DID IT'
– VICTIM

The quotes are a new tweak. They add life to any story. The real characters in a story are always more moving than any reporter's version of events. We know this from TV reportage as much as from newspaper stories which feature actual comments and quoted speech.

DEATH OF
A RAPIST
– VICTIM
STRIKES
BACK

Did you spot the literary/silver screen throwbacks? There's Miller's *Death of a Salesman* and *The Empire Strikes Back* in there somewhere! Finally:

FOODSTORE
RAPIST
KNIFED
BY VICTIM

PROFESSIONAL WRITING TECHNIQUES

Avoid passive constructions, such as 'KNIFED BY', wherever possible. This would be better:

FOODSTORE
RAPIST
KNIFED
IN REVENGE
KILLING

Which do you prefer? Ask yourself 'why?' Then see if you can improve on these didactic efforts.

How a professional 'plays with words'

Study what books, other than this one, say about headings; also categorise the headings you see in papers and magazines. Magazine heads tend to be snappier, cleverer than those found in daily papers for at least two reasons. First, the news may not be funny. And second, the editor working to a tight schedule has much less time to play with words.

The ability to play with words is very highly prized in some quarters. I discovered this early on, as a college student, on the point of getting married and looking for a first job in journalism. Unable to winkle my way into a position on the college rag as a wordsmith (everyone else wanted to be a writer or an editor, and had already staked their claim by the time I arrived) I got in as advertising manager, and proceeded to write on art, music, and all the rest of the topics dear to my heart, having inserted a foot in the door.

With these small writing credentials under my belt, and wise to my penchant for playing with words, punning, and so on, I fixed on *She* magazine as the ideal career entry point. *She* always had the whackiest headings. They were smutty, punny, literary; sometimes crummy, never dull. I ignored the received wisdom that you can't gatecrash national journalism, but have to 'make your bones' on a provincial newspaper first. I always figure that if everyone gangs up to tell the wide world *not* to do something, most people will march to orders and do nothing, leaving less competition for the bold. I sent the editor a letter and was rewarded with an interview.

45

At the interview I was handed a copy of the magazine and asked to give alternative titles and intros to any half-dozen stories; not on the spot, you understand, but at my leisure.

Well, I didn't relax on the hoped-for job; I quickly got on with it. There was one story on Russian intellectual whizz kids. I called that 'Red Hot Kids'. You get the picture. I completed my task in similar vein. A polite letter came back. There was no actual job vacancy, the Ed said, but she would be in touch whenever there was. Six months later I landed a job as a sub-editor on *She*.

I spent 18 months there, playing with words. The play's the thing, when it comes to headings. Here's a recent example. I was writing a column in my syndicated series 'Free Financial Articles by Fleet Street Writers'. This piece was about large mortgages, meaning £500,000 and upwards. I could have called it 'How to Get a Big Mortgage'. But I like my headings to be 'sparkier' than that – and so do the 80 or so editors who receive the column. To find those missing power-words I could have gone to a book of synonyms or metaphors or Roget's *Thesaurus*, or what have you. But I find my own brain twirls rapidly enough, most of the time. I generally make a list that relates to the direction I'm going in. For the mortgage item, it looked like this:

big
large
great
gross
grand
huge
giant
monster
gigantic
fat
fantastic
blockbuster

Here I paused. 'Blockbuster' goes nicely with the word 'borrow'. Editors like alliteration (see page 22). 'How to Borrow a Block-buster of a Mortgage' doesn't work. 'Mortgage' and 'borrow' are windy ways of saying almost the same thing. And if you use just the word 'borrow' you also need to insert the fact that the money is for a 'home loan'. 'Mortgage' is a short-cut way of getting the same message across.

I passed on. What other well-known titles have 'big' in them? This process is a bit like locking on to the literary subconscious!

There's Chandler's book *The Big Sleep* and, of course, F Scott Fitzgerald's *A Diamond As Big As The Ritz*. I knew, then, I was home and dry. The Ritz is a building, if not a house; with just the right sprawntzy ring to it. My title became: 'How To Get a Mortgage as Big as the Ritz.'

That's how I do it. Sometimes the throwaway list of words working towards a title is much longer; sometimes I never hit on something I like; but I can usually produce something that is good enough. Remember: no one knows what you were trying to achieve, how pleased or irked you were with your final offering. As the editorial office will, nine times out of ten, change your best efforts – for the hell of it, if nothing else – don't grow grey hairs over headings. Just be 'good enough'. And nine times out of ten you will be better than you need to be. 'How to Get a Big Mortgage' is not the world's worst heading, by a long shot.

Headings don't need full stops

A heading is an unusual piece of syntax. It can be one word, such as 'Oi!' in a tabloid paper, where the picture tells the story of (for argument's sake) an elephant squirting water over a scantily clad beach beauty; or a phrase – 'Beauty in the Basement' was a title I dreamed up for an article in the *Sunday Times* colour magazine to spotlight the British Museum's policy, at that time, of keeping more works of art below stairs and out of sight than were ever available to the public in the galleries.

The best newspaper heads, it was always drummed into my head as a trainee sub-editor, have verbs in: 'Thatcher Acts to Stem Backbench Revolt', for example. A famous poster sentence dates to World War I where the government cleverly drafted women into the propaganda campaign to keep the cannon fodder coming. 'Women of Britain Say Go!' What they should never have, however, is a full stop. Why not?

The Thatcher heading above is a complete sentence. One of your three Rs will tell you that it should end with a full point. But that's only if you disregard the fact that a headline is a professional 'tool', not a piece of textbook grammar.

A headline is designed to make the reader read on. A full stop tells him or her to stop, or at least slow down. Professional writing is all about generating impetus, excitement. Give a reader a chance to pause for breath, at least in the early stages of reading a piece, and he will fall asleep or turn to something else.

So yes, if you flick through magazines, or scan the poster hoardings, you will see scores of ads where the designer has meticulously dotted his headline. That's his mistake. It happens because designers tend to think of their commercial work as 'works of art', complete in themselves, forgetting the larger purpose of advertising, proselytising, and so on. But that's no reason why we professional writers should.

As advertising guru David Ogilvy says, 'There is no law which says that advertisements have to look like advertisements. If you make them look like editorial pages you will attract more readers. Roughly six times as many people read the average article as the average advertisement.' Since you want to give yourself the best possible fighting chance in the editorial and PR stakes, wear a green eye-shade and run with the *editors*. Headlines in newspapers and magazines *never* have full stops.

Working titles

In a newspaper or magazine office, a story may go right through the editing system wearing nothing more than a working title, perhaps just a label, such as 'Sex Change' for a piece on a woman who became a man.

The pages of the manuscript will be tagged with this working title, as a convenience. Now the curious truth is that, unless you work in an editorial office, and it's your job to give headings to articles, *all* your headings are working titles. You never know whether your choice of title will be the one to appear on the printed page – and 99 times out of 100 it will not be. Why is this?

Any number of reasons. You are less skilled in dreaming up

intriguing titles than the professional editorial wordsmiths and your title falls by the wayside; the sub-editor, who is generally the office 'champ' at headlines, dare not leave well alone, for fear of calling his own existence into question, so comes up with an alternative, which, though inferior, is none the less chosen; your title doesn't fill the available space in the layout design; or some other reason.

One thing we do know, however, is that very often the flavour of your chosen working title lingers on in the final choice of title. Your choice may not be quite right, but it isn't all bad either is how this may be interpreted.

Awaiting a visit from the publisher to discuss my forthcoming book, I wrote scores of alternative titles before dreaming up what I took to be a very good candidate. I also used a piece of psychology to add impact to my final choice of title, in order to get it accepted.

I gave the publisher the also-ran titles printed out as a list on a piece of paper. The ace title I printed on its own in the centre of a plain sheet of white paper. I folded it and placed it inside an envelope. When the publisher had gone through the 'second-best' list, I handed him the sealed envelope, announcing that this was my first-choice title for the book.

Inside the envelope were the words:

Winning
Writing

The publisher was suitably impressed and took my handiwork back to the office. Later, I was told the book was going to be called:

Writing
to Win

My title was good. But it had inspired an even better one. My efforts had been entirely worthwhile.

If you shouldn't dangle your reader, why do so many publications do it?

Have you ever wondered why it is that having been attracted by the title of an article – on the cover of a magazine, in the contents section or even heading up the item itself – you have difficulty tracing the theme of the title in the article, and sometimes fail to find the inspiration for that title altogether?

The reason is subtle. Editorial people are usually only half-trained as writers. They understand angles and how to write striking headings; they know how to pack power into opening sentences, and all the rest of it. But they are less committed to the notion that you must force the reader to read on, which I say is fundamental to *every* aspect of professional writing.

The pity is that editorial folk are not schooled in the harder world of advertising, especially direct mail advertising. Here, if a reader's interest flags, if he fails to get to the 'act now' part of the ad and fill in the coupon, the sale is lost. This discipline can be wonderfully instructive.

In mail order the rules are straightforward enough. You lead with your best shot – the headline contains the most powerful benefit, and also defines your market. Having captured interest, you then restate that theme and/or expand on the benefit. It's simple logic: you've got the reader by the short and curlies, don't loosen your grip by changing tack.

Editorial people disobey this fundamental 'rule' of keep-'em-reading writing not only through ignorance, but also because of a peculiar division of labour on many newspapers and magazines.

In editorial offices the 'creative' duties involved in producing a layout – the designed page as it will appear in print, with pictures, text, and so on – are split. The classic situation is this – and I quote from years of experience.

The sub-editor, an extraordinarily low-status creature, given his responsibilities, is handed a layout, bearing a rough sketch of the page as it will appear, including the columns of print and pictures, together with the original typescript, possibly also the article in printed form for proof-reading, and perhaps a handful of photographs, for which captions need to be written.

At the top of the page, or in some prominent position, the art director, designer, art editor or chief sub-editor, depending on the finance or pretensions of the paper, will have indicated space for a title. He'll show how many lines of copy he would like and also what type style he has chosen for the layout or 'spread'.

This means, of course, that the sub works within formidably tight confines, limited by letter or 'character' count and even grammatical construction, through shortness of the indicated lines of copy. Nevertheless, his brief is to 'find' an intriguing heading and fit it into the available space.

The sub searches through the copy till he finds a good angle, perhaps a striking quotation, a remarkable statistic, or whatever. And he writes a headline around this nugget of information. Quite often, the body of the article itself is sacrosanct. It has been approved by more senior staff, who may even have re-worked the intro – the opening words and sentences – to give it more punch. Though our sub-editor may be expected to 'sub' the article (check for spelling and grammatical errors, re-paragraph, remove libels, and so on) he may have no brief to alter the intro or to re-jig the story to bring up-front the theme of the chosen heading, which would, of course, be the sensible thing to do to ensure continuity of thought.

This, then, is why we so often get a knee-jerk reaction when going from an ace heading to an unconnected first paragraph.

Why does the source of the heading sometimes disappear altogether from the article? This is mainly a newspaper sin. The sub dives into the text and finds his copy gem to craft into a heading, and on the heading goes. Sadly, he has dug too deep, for at a later, critical phase, along comes another sub-editor, whose job is to create space quickly for a more urgent story on the same page, and cuts the piece of copy that yielded the title! 'Cut from the bottom' has always been the rule in newspaper stories, where you start with the hottest tit-bit, such as how much was stolen in a bank raid, and end with what the cleaning lady over the road thought the robbers were wearing in their top pockets.

High-speed manoeuvres are perilous anywhere, it seems – on the road, or on paper.

How to keep 'em reading

'If you're not read, you're dead.' You must have heard that motivating quip before now. Most often it's applied to copywriters producing salesletters or advertisements. But it applies equally vengefully to would-be professional feature writers and PR practitioners. Both direct their work, in the main, to jaded, cynical professionals known as editors.

How do you make your writing unputdownable? First, by understanding the twin elements of readable writing. What you say either needs to be interesting in itself, or it must be made to be interesting. To do this you need to master the writerly devices professionals use to tease and charm their readers into pressing on irrespective of rival demands on their time and attention.

Take a look at this piece of copy. It's as apropos as anything I could choose. It's part of the synopsis and market report I sent the publishers of this book. It worked! It helped to clinch the deal:

> The freelance market is also now busier than ever. With cutbacks on papers, and sizeable redundancy payments, more journalists are relying on their 'mercenary' writing abilities to make a living.
>
> By and large, though, ex-staffers have little enough idea how to operate a writing business profitably and efficiently, and must welcome clear and helpful advice from a Fleet Street professional who is also well versed in PR writing.
>
> Add to this the ranks of industrial professionals – marketing, advertising, communications, personnel executives – not to mention those already working in PR who are told, frequently and accurately, that their press releases are binned nine times out of ten. The universe of book-buyers is wide indeed.
>
> And wider still. The fact is, in many industries, being published in one's particular field brings considerable kudos. Most interesting, though, being published is a high-profile activity for an executive. And a high profile is not a bad thing to have when heads are being hunted . . .

Note, first of all, that the paragraphs vary in size and that they are all *short*. Even professionals (editors, publishers, PR executives, and copy heads in advertising agencies) who are used to spending their time with words are daunted at the prospect of ploughing through slabs of copy, however good a read it turns out to be once they get started.

You know from your own experience that you don't always

quickly appreciate what you later come to enjoy wholeheartedly, whether this be eating oysters, skiing, playing squash, talking in public, and so on. Yet if you had had expert guidance early on, if you had been shown a way of getting started taking small, meaningful steps, one at a time, you might have discovered enjoyment a lot earlier, and got going a lot quicker.

I tried to make this point to a friend who had written a very fine essay which would count towards his teaching degree. I know that traditionally academic writing, being full of its own importance, features slabs of copy. The cockeyed logic seems to be that if all the paragraphs are joined up the writing somehow must be closely reasoned.

I told my student teacher friend I thought his essay was ace, but that 'even fillet steak needs to be cut into small pieces before it can be digested'. The fact that something is always done in a particular way doesn't make it the right way or the best way. Readers like to see some air around writing. It lets them know that soon enough they will be able to pause and take a breather. That's why I prefer short paragraphs and plenty of them.

There is a further subtle point still to be made. Academic essays, when printed up as an academic 'paper', and manuscripts which eventually are turned into books, do indeed have long paragraphs, and will probably continue to have long paragraphs long after I've penned my last piece of prose. What editors, sub-editors and publishers choose to do with copy being prepared for print is their business. You as a contributing, fee-seeking writer need to concern yourself with making your writing easy to take by the first and most important person under whose nose it falls; this is usually the editor or the client.

How to tie your paragraphs together

Good writing often uses thematic connectives, a fancy-sounding name for a simple technique. Hark back to the report on *How to Write Articles for Profit and PR* quoted on page 52. In the first paragraph I talk about redundant journalists. In the second paragraph, I pick up on this theme and refer to 'ex-staffers'. This provides a link between the paragraphs, which lends structure to my reasoning and reassures the reader, who sees that I am still dealing with the same topic.

My second and third paragraphs are also 'welded' together. The third paragraph begins 'Add to this . . . ', reinforcing the notion that this is a closely reasoned document and that the reader should keep reading to appreciate the whole argument, while bearing in mind the previous points.

I mentioned just now that paragraphs one and two of the report on page 52 are linked via a restatement of a theme – journalists without a job. Another way to create a bridge between copy sections, paragraphs, or sentences or phrases, is simply to repeat words. This I do between paragraphs three and four:

> . . . The universe of book-buyers is wide indeed. (End of para 3.)
> And wider still. The fact is, in many industries . . . (Start of para 4.)

Believe it or not, my friend, you are now on the threshold of a major discovery about writing.

Ending the paragraph with the words 'wide indeed' and beginning the subsequent paragraph 'And wider still' is sound technique. The report from which I quote was written fairly fast, and for all that it led to the contract for this book, it was not, of itself, a paid-for piece of work. It was, demonstrably, however, 'good enough'; and that, I suggest, should be your ambition with most of the writing you do, most of the time.

However, there is an easy way to turn this little piece of good writing into very much better copy. All you do is take 'And wider still', and bring it up so that it becomes the *closing* sentence of paragraph three, rather than the opening sentence of paragraph four. The report now looks like this:

> . . . The universe of book buyers is wide indeed. And wider still.
> The fact is, in many industries . . .

Why is this such an improvement? Because 'And wider still' isn't so much a link as a claw.

If I say 'My auntie Jane is fat', that's quite interesting. Suppose, instead, I say 'My auntie Jane is so fat . . . ', and I pause for dramatic effect. The reader is not just interested, he's hanging on my every word. He's dying to know what I'm going to say next. The 'break' in the copy, the space between the paragraphs, is the writerly equivalent of that 'dramatic pause'.

By putting the 'claw' at the end of a paragraph, you virtually guarantee continuing interest; the reader has to read on. Also, and most interestingly, this connective, unlike our previously analysed examples, does not hark *back*. This 'claw' reaches forward. 'And wider still' tells the reader that there is more good news *to come*.

To recap, teasing a reader keeps him reading. Using active connectives that hold out the promise of interesting information also helps to keep his nose pressed against your manuscript.

The same technique holds good for articles. When I first started to syndicate my own material I propositioned Don Wood, Syndication Editor of United Newspapers. There were some 40 papers in the group, including the *Sheffield Star, Yorkshire Post*, and other provincial 'heavies'. Don agreed to take some easy-read articles I'd written on collecting antiques.

One of the first was 'Collecting Cigarette Cards and Other Trade Issues'. It was tightly written and packed with information and amusing anecdotes. Don was mightily impressed and hoped I could keep up the standard. This particular piece had numerous benefits for readers; it introduced them to an interesting hobby that might also enable them to make extra money on the side.

It began:

> You don't need to be a smoker to become a cartophilist – the proper name for a keen cigarette card collector. Anyone with an eye for colour, names or faces, who loves hunting around in junkshops can turn a fascinating hobby into a lucrative pastime.

I had opened with arguably the world's most mesmerising word, 'You'. And I closed my first paragraph with possibly the second most riveting topic, 'Money.' At a stroke, I had appealed to self-interest and self-improvement, two powerful strands worth weaving into any form of writing.

My second paragraph stayed with this money theme:

> Most sought-after of all cigarette cards is the series put out by James Taddy, a tobacco boss who went out of business in 1920.

> Taddy's 'Clowns' – a series of 20 cards – are the 'penny blacks' of card collecting. A fine set can fetch over £2000.

Notice that I didn't 'work my way up' to the 'most sought-after' cards, mentioning more common and far less exciting and valuable Guinea Golds from Ogden, or the Player's series of Dandies. I played my best shot first.

With popular journalism in particular, you can't afford to coast, expecting readers to stay with you, holding their breath waiting for the good bits to come along. They won't. They'll turn the page. Or put on the telly or the kettle.

Having raised the reader's hopes of big killings in cigarette cards, I sustain this euphoria – for a while:

> Perhaps you collected cards as a boy, and you've still got them.

Before becoming rather more realistic:

> But before you rush to your attic or the trunk under the bed for those relics of youth, remember this: creased or grubby cards are not worth a light to the true cartophilist. He prefers his cards in mint condition, and preferably not stuck into a scrapbook.

I now welcome my readers to the club, so to speak:

> As a card collector you'll be in good company. Top comedians Mike and Bernie Winters [this is an old piece . . .] and TV producer John King (he masterminded the famous *Going For a Song* TV show) are all card enthusiasts. It's an investment, and fun at the same time.

I also introduce a very useful and recommended fillip to the narrative: I mention famous names. The point about famous people is everybody knows them without knowing them at all, if you take my point. And there is implied endorsement. The reader is invited to conclude, logically enough, that 'If collecting ciggy cards is good enough for . . . , the wealthy celebrities, surely it could make sense for me, too.' I reinforce this point by reiterating the money theme, this time reworded as 'investment'.

The final paragraph of this 600-word small feature picks up on the money angle, and also looks ahead in an upbeat way:

Tip for the future: Brooke Bond Tea cards are well worth collecting. So, too, are the cards put out by petrol companies and some of the sweet firms in the North. They could be tomorrow's treasures.

The sparky tone has been maintained. Unlike news stories, where information is relayed in a fairly strict order of importance, the tail end reserved for quotes and opinions, features shouldn't fizzle out at the end. Start with a bang, and say goodbye with a bang.

5
Professional Presentation

How to impress an editor face to face

When I was a more active Fleet Street contributor I went out of my way not to see editors. I wasn't shy. Just too busy to 'waste' (as I then saw it) all that valuable work time with actual trips that wrenched me away from my office and typewriter.

I was doing very nicely thank you with 'sales' letters and follow-up phone calls, pulling in, often, more commissions than I could comfortably handle. Indeed, pushing myself hard to meet deadlines and keep all the balls in the air at the same time was part of the excitement. It was a little like famous French 1960s actress Jeanne Moreau's comment on young love. Just turned 40 and looking back on an emotionally active past, she said she could see that one actually enjoyed the complications.

I now accept that it's important to meet editors face to face – for a variety of reasons. No matter how technologically advanced we become, no matter how practical it is even now for people, writers especially, to work from a remote idyll, communicating only by phone, electronic mail and fax, nothing replaces the mysterious personal chemistry that seems to be a vital ingredient in any human transaction – including dealing with editors.

There are practical benefits too. You get more work from editors who meet you, simply because face to face you will spark ideas from each other. On the spot you can develop an idea and encourage 'editor involvement'. An editor who has given a little of himself to an article is more likely to okay the finished item, assuming you follow his suggestions faithfully; and assuming, also, that you have the good business sense to write a quick confirming letter following the meeting, outlining agreed points and summarising the joint conception.

There is a more sinister side, too. No writer-editor relationship endures for ever. Nevertheless, you will enjoy a longer writing life if the editor knows you as a flesh and blood person. Ask yourself this. Which could you more easily stab in the back: a tailor's dummy, or your tailor?

Getting in to see an editor – any editor – is no great shakes. It's one of those select activities that people tell you, with tremendous conviction, even if they've never tried it themselves and don't know anyone who has, that 'it can't be done', or 'you shouldn't do things like that.' Whenever I hear this type of put-off, the sap rises. If this is received wisdom, I tell myself, think of the lack of competition at the gates. Getting in will be a doddle.

Before you start, though, consider this. Editors aren't like you and me. They're more like deity. Or the ruler of Planet X. Benign, possibly, remote, usually... above all, busy. They don't eat people, they like meeting them. Yet they don't get to see many strangers outside their select band of in-house professionals and the coterie of aggressive, prolific writers who feed the national newspapers and magazines. Such writers aren't clubby, however; they are mercenaries. If you want to enjoy similar prestige and fortune you have to muscle into 'their' territory. Go equipped and be prepared.

Know your market

Like most people who are convinced they know what they're doing, editors aren't interested in criticism, not even what we laughingly term 'constructive criticism'. In fact, there is no need to make the slightest comment on the editor's latest issue or a particular blockbuster of a back issue.

Editors aren't dumb. They know that real professional journalists are rarely subscribers to, or even regular readers of, their particular organ. Most journalists simply keep *au fait* with the market. They descend on a big newsagent, such as W H Smith, and buy perhaps £20 worth of papers at a time (requesting a proper receipt, not a till ticket, for tax purposes). The publications are scanned, rather than studied, to pick up the mood of the moment, writing fashions, images, who's writing for whom, and so on.

Editors won't ask questions normally. But if the topic should turn to their own title you'd better be on the ball. So research is essential. One way is to phone the editor's secretary a week or two prior to your appointment. Don't say who you are. Pretend you are doing post-graduate research on anthropomorphism in popular/specialist/women's (whatever applies) magazines, newspapers, or whatever. Ask if you can come in, preferably one lunchtime when the editor will be out and won't see you boning up, and leaf through a stack of back issues. You should also buy as many recent issues as you can find on the shelf and always the very latest copy.

One way to acquire free copies you can cut and mark is to pass yourself off as a potential advertiser (making your fictitious company's goods or services sound as plausible as possible) and ask the ad manager to send you some 'recent back issues, including the current one', plus a rate card. This last part is important; it establishes your apparent bona fides.

Ad people have (or believe they have) something to gain from fulfilling your request. Ask an editorial department for back copies, even offering to pay, and you are just a headache they can do without. They'll promise to oblige but nothing will happen.

So far so good. If you're a serious contender, however, there is more preparatory work to be done. When the rate card comes through, look at the readership profile. Find out who reads the publication, how many readers and purchasers are claimed (not the same thing), how old they are, what they do for a living, what socio-economic category they belong in, how they spend their money, and so on. This should be accurate, honest information – well, as near as you're going to get. Here is a mine of information to help you target article titles that will appeal to these readers.

Ideally, you should do a similar exercise with the opposition, once you know what these titles are. Not all publications have obvious rivals. *Penthouse* took on *Playboy* many years ago, but only a trained eye would know that *Men Only*, while containing similar 'meat', was not really on the same wavelength. You could always go back to the obliging ad manager, having received his 'media pack', thank him, and have a little chat about the perceived opposition. If you can't wheedle a few competitive titles out of him, perhaps you should consider another profession.

You can discover the advertising 'lead-in times' of publications by looking in *British Rate & Data (BRAD* for short). These are the latest dates an advertiser can submit advertising for inclusion in a typical issue. These aren't the same as editorial deadlines. Feature editors and editors' secretaries will supply this unclassified information. Lead-in times are invariably longer than you think, to take account of colour processing, marketing strategy, and so on.

Knowing these dates will help you to come up with suitable article suggestions. For example, you won't suggest a piece on tipples to accompany a barbecue when the magazine is heavily into the January issue and more concerned with the latest variation on mulled wine.

Show you're a tryer

Your best entrée to the editor's office is via a letter and a follow-up phone call. Play a few good shots in the letter (as detailed on page 109). Show that you understand the market and have a feel for the title and readership. Don't fly your own flag in the letter, unless it's very impressive or very relevant, such as you have just been made Vice-Principal of the Leeds College of Fashion and you're suggesting an item on fashion for college students on a budget.

Chase the letter two to seven days later, via a phone call. Have another five or so ideas prepared, which means you can deliver the gist of these in a couple of sentences with the minimum written prompt. Preparing for a phone call to an editor is very like preparing for speaking in public. If you can't rattle off five article outlines from the notes contained on one side of a postcard, you're not ready to talk at all. Practise on a friend or business colleague, using a party line handset. Nothing you say should puzzle your editor or your dopple-ganger friend.

You don't have to hit the spot with any title, but the editor must see that you are a tryer, have thought about his publication, and suspect that you can maintain a flow of ideas. Keep your eye on the ball. Say you have 'A good number of interesting ideas I'd like to go through with you.' You are trying to arrange a live meeting with the ed, not make a killing over the wires.

Getting to see an editor is standard foot-through-the-door sales procedure. Be keen, be smart. Above all, persevere.

'I won't take up more than ten minutes of your time' tells the editor you appreciate his commitments. Don't overdo things: calling it 'valuable time' is over the top. It sounds disingenuous. Besides, your time is valuable too. My time is frequently more valuable than that of editors I meet. But I don't labour that point.

Try to arrange a morning appointment. This may be tricky with newspaper editors, who spend inordinate amounts of time in conference discussing the next issue, post-morteming yesterday's paper, and so on. You might make an early, ie pre-11 am, slot. Avoid afternoon meetings. Most people are more businesslike in the morning, and journalists are with a vengeance, since everything you hear about their lunch-time drinking habits is true and then some.

Lunches are also best avoided, at least in the early stages of a writer-editor relationship. You'll be too on edge to enjoy your food, terrified of downing too much wine, and you won't get much work done, either: a laid table makes a poor work surface.

How to win with what you wear to interviews

What should you wear to your meeting? Should you look wedding-smart? Trendy? Or is genteel poverty more in order . . . something that makes you appear 'hungry for work', and possibly more motivated and reliable? In answer to the question, 'Do clothes make the man or woman?', the answer is no – but they certainly help to make the right impression! So what is the best impression to make on an editor?

I've taught writing skills to young and old, established career people and angry young students. I try this test on them. I take along three briefcases. One is an ancient black leather portfolio, good quality but scuffed at the edges; a large brown Gladstone-type bag in leather-look fabric; and a gleaming black hide Trussardi satchel from Fortnum & Mason. 'Which of these is the best bag to take along to a meeting with an editor?' I ask the class.

Most students don't have a problem with this. They point to the Trussardi. Why? Because it looks the biz. People see a £220 satchel as a reward of success. On balance, people don't display genuine success symbols unless they have earned them and can afford them – we are more honest (or guileless?) than we think. People don't drive around in Lotuses and stint on the family home. They drive a Cavalier and mortgage themselves to the hilt, even though an 'unmerited' status symbol might actually help create a useful impression in their business or profession.

Most of all, my students know, or suspect, that the connection between success and ability is usually real. Of course, an editor would rather work with an established, solvent professional than a beginner who may turn out to be a time-waster who can't deliver the goods. Which is why the Trussardi is the right choice and why certain businesslike clothes are also *de rigueur* for interviews.

For men
A dark blue, charcoal grey, possibly mid-grey suit is best. Grey flannel is okay, stripes are so-so. Black, while fine for a lady, looks funereal on a man. Rustic colours (brown, burgundy, green, cream, tweed etc) are out, as are checks, Prince of Wales or otherwise, sports jackets and blazers, unless you are a member of a truly prestigious club, such as the Olympic. Braces are best worn out of sight. Where trousers have belt loops, use them.

The best shirt is plain white, not even a self-stripe or pattern, with classic spearpoint or cutaway collar. Plain pastel blue is okay, stripes are dubious – they spell 'City' and that may work against you. Ties are dark blue or dark red, or a mix of both, totally unostentatious, entirely silk and probably expensive.

No bangles, ID bracelets, medallions (visible over or under your shirt), ear-rings, nose pins or tie clips. Shoes are black or dark blue leather, laced or slip-on, never suede. No snaffles, tassels, miniature brass horse-bits, silver tips, Cuban heels, chukka boots, or two-tone tap-dancers. Shoes, by the by, are always worn polished.

Lightweight lisle or mercerised cotton socks, in plain black or dark blue or grey are okay. Self-patterned, yes; socks with clocks, no.

For women

A neat, dark suit with a plain silk blouse in a contrasting pastel colour is advised. No trousers, miniskirts or the slightest suggestion of casualness or frippery. Male editors like a woman to look like a woman – draw your own conclusions. But female without fuss. A slight ruffle to the edge of a crisply pressed shirt, or a dark bow tie, can help to relieve an otherwise sombre business outfit, which should always be of a natural fibre – wool, cotton or silk. Man-made materials have a metallic look which radiates second-rate.

Wear lipstick and eye make-up, but remember that under artificial light face make-up can look caked. Nails should be carefully filed and varnished with clear if not coloured lacquer. Clean, brushed, natural-look hair is best; leave the rainbow look to those who work outdoors. Legs can be bare only if tanned, otherwise stockings or tights are a must.

Jewellery is costly, not costume, or not worn at all. Shoes, belts, handbags and other accessories are all of a piece, matching or complementing each other as stylishly and discreetly as possible.

Cuttings that cut the cackle

Actual writing credentials are established largely by osmosis. Via those printed on your letterhead – no one ever doubts these, in the same way as bosses rarely verify claimed academic qualifications; it's all taken on trust. Nor do editors normally show the slightest interest in your cuttings though, of course, you must take them along, just in case.

On this tack, never ask an editor (or anyone in a position of power) to read something while you watch and wait. It must be something to do with bad potty training, but few people can do this successfully. They exhibit displacement activity, fail to concentrate or forget what they read. I never met anyone who was other than uncomfortable about this impromptu 'test'.

Now, although editors rarely ask to see cuttings, and won't read them if they do, it will pay you to impress them should this happen. The way to do this is to 'blow up' your cuttings. I had a professional photographer turn my best cuttings into bromides –

huge photographic prints. These look pristine practically forever, they don't mark when handled, and being oversize they impress like mad. PS. Don't forget to include the masthead of the magazine or newspaper in which they appeared, and the date – if this helps your case.

As well as your minimum five article ideas – made up to this number with fresh material, if you got the slightest hint of an anti-reaction when any were mooted over the phone to the editor when you arranged your interview – you should always float one or more ideas for a *column*. As my mother never ceases to tell me, if you don't ask you don't get. It's got to be worth a crack; it could be the making of you.

Money talks. So always talk money

Always talk money – and always know what you're talking about. What you consider fair pay for your work is irrelevant; what matters is what you can get – or are likely to be offered. Wouldn't you kick yourself to discover you'd been paid £20 for doing work regularly rated at £200? You should know what you would want for the job, as a minimum, and also know what the going rate is for the paper or magazine. This is easier said than done.

The various 'trade' associations – National Union of Journalists (NUJ), Society of Authors, Public Relations Consultants Association, Institute of Public Relations, and so on – are all helpful, though you might have to show some real cunning to pull this information if you aren't a member. A promise to join, and a request for membership papers works well, as I recall. The NUJ publishes an annual booklet on freelance minimum rates.

Best of all, waste no time in finding and cultivating a friend in the business. Inside information is the best, and favourites and well-established writers always command higher pay cheques, regardless of the quality of the work. If you must improvise, through ignorance, tell an editor 'your usual rates will be acceptable.' If the editor asks you what you think they are, turn this round: 'Sounds as if these may have changed. You'd better tell me what they are these days.' If the ed says he doesn't have 'usual rates', he's a liar and a cad (and not much of a mathematician either), and should you be working for such a person?

Always ask for expenses. I use a variety of words which help to soften the body blow this usually seems to be – though why a writer should be out of pocket by a cent is a puzzle to me. Accordingly, I ask for 'basic/justifiable/unavoidable/agreed/nominal/verifiable/billed/out-of-pocket/working expenses'.

Having clinched a deal, discussed payment, word count, deadline, illustrations, angles, and so on, don't run off and start research and writing. Go home and write a letter confirming all these points (see Chapter 8). Document the progress of your assignment by means of letters to the editor, especially changes in wordage, slant etc.

Above all, try your damnedest to meet deadlines. Reliable jobbing writers stay in business longer than brilliant erratic ones.

Copyright is your right to hold on to the long-term value in your writing

Copyright is an intricate subject. Most writers and PR people rub along nicely enough without knowing all the ins and outs of copyright. It's like driving a car and not knowing how the engine fits together. It's fine until the car breaks down. Then you wish you knew a bit more.

Copyright problems are best avoided. To do this you must know the ground rules. When a writer creates a piece of writing he owns the copyright in that work, unless he does it as part of his paid employment, when the copyright is automatically the property of his employer. There is no copyright in ideas, only in 'fleshed out' ideas. There is, therefore, copyright in a synopsis. If someone comes along and publishes your written work without permission, or uses your synopsis, that is a breach of copyright and actionable in law.

Copyright relates to the right to trade in writing (and photographs, etc), and also the right to reproduce such creative offerings. Most magazines and newspaper writing should, strictly speaking, be sold with the letters FBSR (First British Serial Rights) appended. These letters should appear on the manuscript and be mentioned in prior correspondence.

The granting of copyright operates in favour not of the publisher but of the author. It's similar to what the computer industry terms a 'default activity'. It is assumed that only this minimal licensing right of FBSR is granted in the absence of some other copyright agreement.

FBSR allows first use in a periodical publication within UK territories. When you sell a piece to a national magazine and offer FBSR, the editor will assume that this piece has never before appeared in print in a similar form in a similar publication.

There is also an unwritten 'law' that says that you will not allow your work to be published in a similar medium for up to perhaps three or six months following its original publication, this being the 'active life' of a magazine, less for a newspaper.

In the normal way, a writer undertakes a radical re-write, adds fresh material, and the 'same' article may appear the very next day or even concurrently. You just need to be good at plagiarising your own work.

If you decided to include the article in a symposium, or read it out on the radio or turn it into a TV play, these would be outside the scope of FBSR. Use in these other media could occur before or after printed publication.

You might want to mention in a book that such a piece was due to appear or had already appeared in such and such a magazine, or newspaper, out of courtesy; there is, however, no statutory obligation.

The National Union of Journalists had a rule of thumb that gave writers some kind of protection against editors who commissioned work on an FBSR basis and then sat on it, preventing the writer from offering subsidiary rights. The NUJ said that any work not published after six months (even if paid for) could be offered elsewhere on an FBSR basis.

The point to remember is that the author/writer is the proprietor of all his various copyright options as an absolute right. He may sell or lease these as he wishes.

In the bad old days magazines were forever commissioning articles for UK publication and then retailing them round the world via their own syndication wings or an independent syndication agency. When the original payment arrived there was a little note indicating that 'all rights' or 'world rights' had mysteriously been purchased, unbeknown to the writer. Occasionally there was a cash sweetener included, or an offer for the syndication privilege.

One leading magazine publisher used to require writers to endorse cheques. The message printed on the backs of these cheques entitled the publisher to enjoy all rights by dint of encashment! It may still happen but you don't have to accept this or any similar ploy and the law will uphold your right not to be bound by this kind of blackmail.

Photography has its own copyright rules and mores. The simple working rule is that if the photographer buys the film he also owns the copyright – a good reason not to include the cost of the 'raw materials' of photography in your bills.

There are many complications with copyright, as you can appreciate. When the going gets tough, I consult my copy of *Copyright* by R F Whale (Longman). Another useful book on the subject is *A Handbook of Copyright in British Publishing Practice* by J M Cavendish (Cassell).

6
PR Writing – For Yourself and Other Clients

How to write a brilliantly effective press release

The press release is the most accessible form of publicity available to most people in most businesses. Anyone can concoct their own little story and mail it out to editors and news 'tasters' in TV and radio stations. You don't have to be a professional; and one of the things journalists quickly discover is that most people who write press releases aren't. Even PR people who are paid, usually quite handsomely to write the things, frequently don't know much about how to make them work. Which explains why press releases have a very high mortality rate.

There are many myths about press releases. Received 'wisdom' says that a press release should ideally be no longer than one page of typed, double-spaced copy. Even news editors I've interviewed on the topic make that point. I say tosh. What they mean is something quite different.

Since the great majority of press releases are uninteresting, irrelevant to the publication, out of date, badly put together etc, editors naturally prefer them to be brief since this saves scanning time and they can be binned that much quicker. But faced with an interesting, usable release, the editor is *hungry* for information.

Insiders know this, if they give the topic half a thought, because press handouts, when used, are very often printed more or less verbatim. Now if the story is good enough to be used as it is, at least one factor restricting the length of the story you've planted –

there are others, such as available space, overall newsworthiness, and so on – is the brevity of the item.

I don't send out press releases for the sake of it. It's a waste of my time and my clients' money. I construct them so that they at least have a fighting chance of being used, and that often, but not always, means they run to two and sometimes three or four pages.

Even the double-spacing stipulation is off target. If cost is a factor, you can 'telescope' your story into one folio of paper by using one-and-a-half spacing. This still gives the sub-editors room to insert their alterations.

I very often send out press stories on my own normal headed paper, as used for letters, bills, and so on. Well-designed letterheads are an important part of your work-getting armoury, as I explain at greater length in Chapter 7. Whatever makes headed paper work will also help your cause with press releases, unless you can afford to have different, equally striking paper printed just for releases.

Do you need 'run-on' sheets? A run-on sheet is normally a near blank piece of paper, with some design element that relates to the full-blown letterhead design. As everyone in this business is at pains to ensure that pieces of paper that get separated in an editor's office can easily be returned to their rightful place, the most sensible course is to use the complete and original letterhead for every page of your press release.

A reader of my last book made a good point about my own letterhead. He said having a printed list of 'credentials' down the left-hand margin gave subs a headache, as this is the traditional place for marking up the copy for the printer. He's right, and I'm grateful for the tip. I'll do something about it when I've used up the 4000 sheets of microperforated (for computer printout) letterhead I've just had done.

How to supercharge your press releases

Press releases need all the help they can get. They are the literary equivalent of the B movie. Everyone expects them to be second-rate, and they rarely disappoint. The trouble is, even those that are interesting, well constructed, relevant to the publication at which they are aimed etc, will still get looked at disdainfully, dutifully, through force of habit.

This is why it pays to gain a reputation as a PR whose releases are well written, fun to read, informative, and so on. This has a cumulative effect. Your stock will soar in editorial offices and you could develop that most useful attribute of a PR operative, a *relationship*, so that the editor or a staff writer actually comes to you for stories, expert comment, perhaps from your client, and so on.

Press releases therefore require you to have at your fingertips the entire panoply of journalistic/writerly tricks of the trade. Should a press release be easy to read? How quickly do you want it binned?

Part of my regular work involves writing about the antiques fairs scene. I also work as a publicity consultant for the organisers of many of the most important antique shows, such as the London Antique Dealers Fair, the West of England Antiques Fair, the Decorative Antiques and Textiles Fair, and others.

As a correspondent I am on the receiving end of numerous, mainly tedious and poorly put together, press releases. I also issue press releases by the hundreds on behalf of my own clients. I see where others fall down, and make sure I keep my own hit rate up. It's an ideal situation for a writer and I suggest you aspire to it.

Mostly, press releases issued by PRs working for fairs organisers content themselves with being 'reference material', though the writers may not be aware of this dismal fact. In other words, they give the date, time and place of an event, useful only to the news editor with an empty diary, and some well-chosen hyperbole about how many millions of pounds the antiques will be worth collectively, with perhaps something of real interest to a handful of readers – the fact that the show is being opened by a local dignitary or a stage or screen star who happens to have inherited a few watercolours.

My ambition and brief is usually to hit the nationals with something they will consider worth using. It's rarely an easy task. But it obviously helps to know where news editors and picture editors are coming from. On page 73 you'll see the eye-catching composite picture I sent to over 100 newspaper editors. It shows a rare and valuable 'planter's chair' and leggy model Sharon doing her best to find the most comfortable position, given the chair's bizarre construction.

I knew the picture would grab attention, at least with male recipients, and I used the release to direct their attention straight back to it with the title:

HOW DO YOU SIT COMFORTABLY ON A PLANTER'S CHAIR? SOLVE THE PUZZLE AT THE DECORATIVE ANTIQUES AND TEXTILES FAIR AT THE HOTEL RUSSELL, LONDON WC1, 9-11 MARCH 1988

Most news and picture editors on the nationals don't give a Daiquiri about a planter's chair, or indeed about antiques, except from the 'superlative' point of view; for example, the most expensive Breguet watch, the highest price a Van Gogh has ever fetched at auction, the newly discovered Watteau, and so on.

What they do go for, mainly in the tabloids, is attractive female form, and also, of course, anything with strong 'picture potential'. The planter's chair has this rare attribute in vast measure.

The picture is itself a puzzle. It poses all sorts of questions: what sort of chair is it? What are those flaps for? How do you sit on it? Do you put your legs on the flaps? And so on. All those thoughts are prompted by the curious look of the thing, which is why people say a picture is worth a thousand words.

The best pictures need few words

But I am not in the business of peddling just pictures to newspapers in this instance. My job is to get my client's name and, more important, the date of his event prominently featured in a story in the paper, which was why I also 'voiced' these questions in my body copy:

How do you relax in a planter's chair, the ultimate no-holds-barred recliner? What is the purpose of those massive wooden flaps that swing out from under the arm-rests?

The picture is the tantalising free gift, the 'loss leader' that grabs the editor by the lapels and gets him reading my story.

I say loss leader advisedly. This was the most complicated

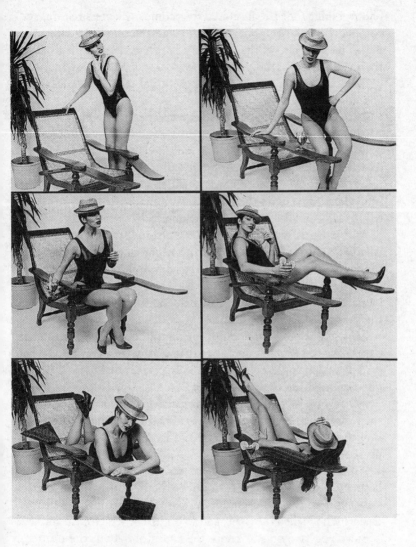

Figure 1. *How do you sit comfortably on a planter's chair?*
I was promoting the Decorative Antiques and Textiles Fair.
The antique trade papers might feature a bureau-bookcase or a chaise-longue picture sent out with a press release. The nationals need livelier encouragement, hence the composite picture of model girl Sharon trying to get to grips with the nineteenth-century teak planter's chair. What do you do with those flaps? All is revealed on pages 74-5.

photographic shot I'd organised to accompany a press release, and complications cost money. There was the shooting cost, the model fee, the hire of the 'planter's hat' (even that came to £6!), the printing cost (the prints measure 11 × 9.5in), special size hard-backed envelopes, as well as the usual targeting, packaging and postage costs.

This picture was also a loss leader in another more technical sense. Although the composite is large, the six individual views measure only 5 × 4in each, far smaller than most newspaper offices prefer for reproduction purposes. Mainly they 'blow up' black-and-white prints to at least 10 × 8in and preferably 10 × 12in, since the more detail and clarity there is in the original, the better the eventual, usually smaller, newsprint version.

And journals work, for preference, from 'original' prints: the enlarger shines a light through the negative and the print that results is an original. Because of the complications of the planter-with-model shot, a copy negative had to be made of the six assembled views, with the result that the definition suffered slightly in the submitted composite shots.

This might be good enough for reproduction in a local newspaper office on a low budget, or a magazine with a very good print system which could enhance the copy print, but it would not be good enough for a top newspaper.

What's more, the picture editor and his lensman might have their own ideas on how best to pose Sharon on the chair and, as I say, they would want to work from large, original bromides or prints.

Although the paper would, of course, fund the cost of this bespoke photo session, there might be client time involved, or Mel Lewis might have to organise the model, the props, the antique dealers who loaned the chair, and so on. All of which costs money.

Since you're dying to know the true story about the planter's chair, I can tell you, as I told about 150 editors, that

Model Sharon tried using the flaps as a drinks table, a foot rest, a head and an arms support – even if the latter did mean turning turtle!

Another convincing theory? 'To stop termites and scorpions

climbing up their legs, planters used to hook their feet over the flaps,' according to antique dealer, Eric Gunawardena.

Mr Gunawardena, a partner in Roderic Antiques of Church Street, Kensington, bought a number of these mid-Victorian curiosities over from his native Sri Lanka – especially for this fair.

Roderic Antiques is one of 62 dealers exhibiting at the famous Decorative Antiques and Textiles Fair at the Hotel Russell, Russell Square, London WC1, from 9-11 March 1988.

It was a neat way of getting around to antiques *per se*, and the event I was promoting. Incidentally, it pays to repeat important information in a press release. The date was crucial, clearly. And yes, it was in the title, but titles get glanced at, rather than absorbed. Besides, the heading is in capital letters, and caps are always harder to read; we're simply less used to them.

Do press releases need illustrations?

Do fish need water? Let me try to explain how I feel about pictures and images generally.

The other day I was walking through the town of Chippenham. Many of the shops had sales on. As usually happens, not only do prices go down, but so too does the standard of window display. It's easy enough to understand why: the goods in the window may eventually be pulled out of the window and sold, so there's no point dressing them up.

Interestingly, one store selling carpets had mounted a stunning display. It was a giant-size fist covered in some kind of red carpet material. The fist appeared to be smashing through the glass and, of course, there was talk of shattered prices, and so on. I don't know how good the deals were. But I do know that the fist display grabbed me by the lapels and made me look.

Now consider this point about newspapers. Whatever you think about the quality, morals or even the design of tabloid newspapers like the *Sun*, the *Daily Mirror*, the *Star*, *Today*, and so on, there isn't a scrap of doubt that they outsell more ponderous papers, like *The Times*, the *Daily Telegraph* etc. The way tabloids look obviously gives them huge popular appeal and a commercial edge.

Now answer this question. On tabloid papers, which has greater prominence – the words or the pictures? The headlines may have poster-size letters, but they contain few enough words and the story that follows generally won't count for much space.

But that's what tabloids are all about, I hear you say. They are all about images, as opposed to deep thought and carefully reasoned text. Exactly! And that is their strength. Very often the pop dailies lead with the same story, and the main difference will be the photograph used on the cover. The paper that sells best is very often the one with the most striking picture.

Finally, consider the adage that clothes make the man. In the film *My Fair Lady*, when Eliza Doolittle, the scrawny cockney sparrow, is dressed up like a lady, she looks every inch the aristocracy she isn't. More recently, in the movie *Trading Places*, Eddie Murphy (of *Beverly Hills Cop* fame) is taken literally off the streets, where he's a beggar pretending to be a limbless Vietnam war veteran, and clothed in standard issue Wall Street livery – dark suit, white shirt, autumn fruit colour silk tie. He looks the part without uttering a word. And that's the point here: images work faster than words.

Editors scan press releases. Their radar systems are highly developed, so they don't spend much time deliberating on what are, after all, unsolicited, totally biased contributions. Therefore, it must pay you to 'zap' editors as quickly as possible.

You know to do this with an attention-getting headline. Wherever possible, you should also use a striking image.

There are subsidiary benefits, in addition. A second-rate story may get into print on the strength of a good picture. Press pictures are also freebies – never underestimate the power of 'free', especially with papers on a low budget. And your quality 10 × 8in or 6 × 4in shot is there, ready to be used. An editor may need an image to fill a space quicker than his own photographer can supply it, and again the right PR picture scores.

What makes a good publicity image?

Not necessarily what clients or PR people would like it to be, is the short answer.

The businesslike client would like the picture to show the product – isn't that the most interesting object in the world? The egotistical client wants his or her portrait to go out with a press announcement. The lazy PRO doesn't give a damn either way, as long as the release gets sent and his bills get paid.

The answer, my friend, isn't 'blowing in the wind'. It's locked up in what Hercule Poirot calls those 'little grey cells'.

Most press releases are just pieces of letterheaded paper with text on. Some have accompanying photographs. What we do know is that most releases are poorly produced (written, targeted, timed etc) and most enclosed illustrations aren't worth reproducing. However, the purpose of submitting a picture with a press release is not necessarily to get that picture used in the paper or magazine. The image is primarily intended to 'raise the profile' of your press release. To make it 'leap out at the eye', something which, according to the editor of Londoner's Diary in the *Evening Standard*, rarely happens.

I had a client on a low budget. I knew the release we were planning to send would lose itself on the editor's desk without an eye-catching accompanying photograph. Yet there was no money available for pictures.

I searched around on my shelves and found a book with an image that would suit our purposes. The release was intended to summon press photographers to a photocall. The book was a guide to taking better photographs and one illustration was a silhouette of a man holding a camera properly, to avoid camera shake.

I took the book down to the local instant print shop. I copied the picture, in various sizes, using the reducing facility, and took the selection of images back to my office.

Settling on a size that would suit the letterhead to be used for the release, I cut round the silhouette and stuck this template down on to a blank piece of paper. This sheet would become my 'master copy'.

The diminutive photographer was pasted down at a jaunty angle in the left-hand margin, cutting into the opening paragraph and the headline. Using the image obliquely made it leap off the page that little bit more than if it had been set down square to the edge of the page. I word-processed the copy to fit snugly round the cut-out shape of the silhouette.

When the master was overprinted (photocopied) on to letterheads, the image was certainly eye catching. It also relayed my message, at a glance, that this news item was of interest to press photographers in particular. Most important of all, of course, the wheeze had cost my client next to nothing.

One small point. You can't go filching images from books willy nilly. Illustrators have rights as well as wordsmiths. My understanding is that copyright in book illustrations is the same as for authors. It continues – or 'subsists', in copyrighting jargon – during the lifetime of the author/illustrator until the end of the period of 50 years from the end of the calendar year in which the author/illustrator dies. To be on the safe side, you should ask for permission to use any published image and get the all-clear in writing before proceeding. PS. There may be a fee to pay.

Good images don't fall off trees – or do they?

Here's another picture problem. I was working for Cristina Stuart, head of Speakeasy, a company specialising in teaching speaking and presentation skills. Speakeasy was about to take a stand at an important exhibition and wished to use the event as a news peg to announce its services to the press.

We decided to send out a photocopy of a portrait of Cristina, rather than an actual photographic print, to save money. We inserted the line: 'Call Speakeasy (01-346 2776) for a print of the portrait of Cristina Stuart (photocopy enclosed).' This saves on costs, but also lets the editor know there is a photograph available. When the call comes through, you move heaven and earth to get the print to that editor quickly, needless to say, by motor cycle messenger, Datapost or DIY.

PR WRITING – FOR YOURSELF AND OTHER CLIENTS

But this didn't get round my self-imposed creative 'discipline' of getting some sort of image on to the actual text of the press release, which in this case was to be Cristina's own headed paper. The flavour of the message was peculiarly personal, as you will read.

What image would work? Just prior to the Speakeasy assignment, I had sent out a mailing on behalf of an antiques fair organiser. We had used a truly riveting image of a seventeenth-century hardwood nutcracker, carved in the shape of a man's head, the 'jaw', operated by a handle at the back of his neck, being the part that cracks open the nut. Anthropomorphic images are always good to use, and this one had a staring eye and pained mien that exactly suited our purpose.

I referred to my adaptation of the image in the headline and picked up the theme in my opening sentence:

IS THIS HOW YOU FEEL WHEN ASKED TO SPEAK IN FRONT OF PEOPLE?
The good news for the tongue-tied is that speaking in public can be learnt – painlessly, quickly, inexpensively. I'll be showing how on the stand of my company Speakeasy at the Barbican Centre, London, in April (details overleaf).
Speakeasy started quietly enough . . .

And so on, into my spiel. The release was written in the form of a letter, and ended, as every sales letter should, with a PS. The opening words of a letter and the PS. are the best-remembered parts of a business letter, say researchers. Ours said:

PS. I'll be sending you a copy of my new leaflet, '25 Steps Towards Speaking With Confidence'. Reproduce it as you wish. There will be no charge.

I also inserted a PPS which served as a caption to the nutcracker image:

PPS. Tongue-tied symbol top right is a seventeenth-century nutcracker.

You should never puzzle your reader with your writing by, for example, posing questions you don't quickly answer – and you shouldn't dangle them with mysterious images, either.

Caption writing for publicity pictures, by the way, is something of an art form. Of course, every picture must have a caption. Ideally, the press release carries the caption, and the back of the picture also has a caption. This enables the picture to be identified and enables the sub-editor to mark up the caption for the printer. I like to write long captions, like the one for the antique planter's chair adorned with a leggy model (see page 73):

> HOW DO YOU SIT ON A PLANTER'S CHAIR? Model Sharon shows how. Planters were British expatriate tea and rubber growers. These chairs are Sri Lankan, from the second half of the nineteenth century. Example depicted is teak; more typically they are heavier paduk wood, with rattan seating.
>
> This chair is priced at £450, one of several being sold (from £320) by Roderic Antiques at the Decorative Antiques and Textiles Fair at the Hotel Russell, Russell Square, London WC1, 9-11 March 1988. *More information:* 01-624 5173/01-624 1787; or 0379 852777 (publicity).

Why such a long caption? Two very good reasons. I happen to know that pictures get separated from their story in editorial offices. And also that interesting images are often preserved in a file, long after a press release has bitten the dust. The long caption gives my client two bites at the cherry.

How to embargo your press release

Issuing press releases enables companies to manage their own news output. Through people like me, clients can shape and direct information. They can also time when their stories go out to the media, something which can prove crucial to a campaign. A press release subject to a timing restriction is said to be embargoed. Managing the timing of a press release, by means of the embargo system, is a little understood technique – especially by PR people who have no direct experience of life in a busy newspaper office.

Abuses
While slapping an embargo on a release may appear to give it instant cachet and urgency, many journalists view embargoes with

a jaundiced eye. Too frequent, irresponsible and manipulative use of the system may even be counter-productive.

Abuses include issuing an embargoed story to pre-empt the story being published from an alternative, legitimate source, when the latter would be inconvenient to management, or embargoes which are restricted in such a way as to thwart a particular media office.

However, correctly and sparingly used, the embargo is a powerful weapon in the PR armoury. These are typical (and acceptable) instances of when to embargo a release:

1. When the story is long and complicated, such as an official report. The more time the reporter has to absorb the message and research round it, the better coverage you are likely to receive. White Papers and government reports make extensive use of embargoes.

2. When a release includes the text of a speech. Most speeches are far from spontaneous, but to have a verbatim report appear quickly in the press smacks of stage management. So you might restrict publication to the evening of the day of a speech, enabling the morning papers to carry the story, but not the evening papers on the speech day itself.

3. For dramatic impact. A surprise guest at a press do will cease to be a surprise if the story gets out in advance. So the press are informed and invited, but the story is embargoed until the event itself. Bear in mind, though, that events themselves cannot be embargoed; you cannot hold up a report until *after* the event. TV and radio are entitled to cover events as of right – and the same applies to a speech, once it is being made.

4. To choose the best time for publication. The Sunday press, with its acres of print and 'ruminative' style of reportage, is a good place to lose a good story. Which is why some releases are embargoed for Sunday, to by-pass that day and aim for Monday publication, when competing news may be minimal. Financial clients in particular are often at pains to avoid publication of 'sensitive' figures in the evening press, and insist on a time which gives the morning papers first crack at the information.

The actual time you put on your embargo – normally expressed as NOT FOR PUBLICATION UNTIL ... NOT FOR USE UNTIL ... or, more simply, EMBARGOED ... followed by the time, day and date – is of crucial importance. Long embargoes are alienating. Newspaper people largely run off adrenalin, so anything that says 'hold fire' is demotivating.

Learn lead-in times
Then there's the risk that scraps of paper disappear, or are filed out of sight and mind. Worst of all, your release sent out on Monday and embargoed for Thursday may actually straddle the press day of a regional weekly, so you really will lose friends and antagonise people.

You need to know when stories are put together in a newspaper, radio or television office, and what their lead-in times are. If in doubt, pick up the phone and find out. Thus a release pegged to a 6 pm embargo will miss the local evening paper and the local evening news section of regional television. Whereas a noon embargo misses local radio stations and their liveliest morning audience and also the morning paper, but you are in with a better chance for evening TV and evening press.

A more simple way to embargo stories, without labouring the point in print, is to use a hand delivery service to media offices. Simply ask the despatch company to send your release out to arrive at a particular time.

A checklist of press release 'musts'

Writing a first-class press release is no great shakes, even for a beginner. There are ground rules. The rest, the 'dream topping', the part that leaps off the desk and grabs an editor by the throat, is up to you, your imagination and motivation. The rest of this chapter will help in this respect. Meanwhile, the nitty gritty.

Every press release must have:

1. A date.
2. A title.
3. White space around the text and between the lines of text.

4. Clear indication that 'more follows'. I also like 'pto'.
5. A 'catchline' – a word or two that recalls the title, followed by a number. The second page of this story could read 'Checklist 2'.
6. The word 'ENDS' at the end.
7. Names and phone numbers that editors can contact for more information. Someone should be reachable round the clock.
8. Picture captions.

There is more, much more. The Who, What, Why, When, Where and How of your release must be quickly relayed. A release contains facts and also a good quote from a VIP working for your client, or a comment from an independent. If you want to put a time restriction on your press release, embargo it.

How to target a press release

Here's how I approached press release targeting for a very new assignment. The client runs a classy restaurant in a major tourist-trap town. He is about to sell up and move to a more rural setting near by – a magnificent period mansion with grounds, fountains, swimming pool, accommodation, and so on. The plan, backed by substantial funding, is to turn this into an upmarket restaurant with hotel and conference facilities.

For the first client meeting I need to have at my fingertips a checklist of carefully researched mailing options. This should be a straightforward enough task. It rarely is.

Never omit the 'thesaurus stage'. Everyone has a thesaurus; it's called a brain. Let it whirl for a bit, and do a bit of prompting as well. I refer to my copy of PNA *Media Guide*, published by PNA six times a year (see page 161). This is the most up-to-date media reference I know. I look under all sorts of heads: Food, Hotel, Catering, Conference, Cookery, and even Gardening, since the restaurateur/manager plans to develop a cottage garden and grow rare herbs.

The list now looks like this:

National newspapers
Regional and local newspapers
County magazines
Lifestyle magazines (*World of Interiors, House & Garden* etc)
Consumer magazines (*Family Circle, Woman's Realm*)
Trade publications (under all the headings I've researched)
TV and radio, local and national.

PNA *Media Guide* gives phone numbers, addresses and names of editors, correspondents, and so on. To be totally on the ball with media and personnel changes I can use PNA direct – they prepare, stuff and send out the release; or, if I have an IBM compatible computer with hard disk, I can transmit, check and clear releases for despatch by PNA, via the electronic form of the guide, known as PNA Targeter.

A card index will also serve. But you may need to phone to check that your hard data is still accurate. Limited run DIY mailings can be very effective. The trick is to improvise and do it, rather than be obsessional, worry about the cost of it all, and fail to act.

How to promote your business via 'sponsored' articles

As we have seen, a press release, at best, relays interesting information, relevant to the editor's publication. It also features an element of news.

News is a flexible commodity, as you discovered in Chapter 4. A company may introduce a new line, expand its premises, take on new staff, lower prices, even raise prices – all are potentially newsworthy items in the right hands, and could provide 'meat' for a press release. Or an event, such as taking a stand at a trade fair, will furnish an opportunity to telegraph a newsworthy promotional message via a press release.

The problem is, it's easy to overdo it. Press release distribution house PNA tell me that some of their clients issue four press handouts a week. How do they do it? How do they afford it? It's not a cheap exercise. Where does all the 'news' come from?

The answer is that the multinationals who mount press campaigns of such intensity have the wherewithal and enough divisions to generate a constant flow of news. Presumably, they also have the wit to create sufficiently varied 'paper' personalities for their various departments, via a selection of news release stationery with minimal family likeness. You'd be surprised how many companies don't have enough nous to skirt creatively round this minor dilemma.

But what about lesser mortals, such as you, me, and my clients? We probably don't have enough news, or news pretexts. As they say in the PR business, it's all about column inches. Is there some way to keep up the pressure, so to speak, without becoming obtrusive? The pushy PR person is as much a stereotype as the booze-swilling journalist.

I have found a way. Sponsored articles. In other words, regular articles, backed by a client, which promote that client, but with sufficient general interest to overcome the anxiety that readers will view such pieces as purely promotional vehicles.

In fact, potentially there may also be internal resistance to overcome. The advertisement manager may view this type of sustained PR activity as potentially lost revenue for his own department. If the client wasn't getting so much free exposure, he might be buying advertising space, the ad manager argues. The intelligent editor replies that the paper is making money by saving money – they would have to pay a top-class writer a serious amount of money for a regular series of well-written, carefully vetted articles.

Against this tricky commercial and ethical background one thing is crystal clear: mounting and sustaining such an operation is not for amateurs. The articles need to be as carefully written as the 'offer' announcement that launches the scheme.

Here is the letter I wrote to 800 editors on behalf of my client, the Porchester Group, now better known as the giant financial services conglomerate, the MI Group:

Dear Editor

FREE FINANCIAL ARTICLES BY
FLEET STREET WRITERS

As you probably know, The Porchester Group, the well-known insurance broking company, is teaming up with

Cornhill (sponsors of Test cricket for many years) to form a new financial services group.

The exact name and shape of that organisation will be announced very soon. Meanwhile, one service that Porchester would like to establish right now is to offer house journal editors, like yourself, the chance to run lively financial articles.

These articles are yours to use free of charge.

As you can appreciate, the idea is very new. And articles are FREE. All that is asked is that the line 'Compiled with the assistance of The Porchester Group' is added at the foot of each article (or elsewhere).

Porchester has offices in London (City and West End), Birmingham, Bristol, Liverpool and Manchester. Where possible we will add the town appropriate for you and a local phone number to help your readers locate their nearest branch.

I have enclosed one of the most compelling titles – 'RETIRING? ONE WAY TO GET CASH FROM YOUR HOME WITHOUT MOVING OUT.'

This piece is yours to use once you confirm your interest quickly, using the enclosed envelope and reply form attached.

We are currently adding a new title every week. Naturally we would prefer you to use the articles on a regular basis and I'll be pleased to send you every title to give you plenty of choice, regardless of how often your publication appears. However, please say how frequently you will be able to run the articles on that reply form.

To help us give you the best possible service, please circle the options listed on the folio attached. Then get your secretary to send it back to me right away, if you will, in the self-addressed envelope provided, together with a compliments slip or letterhead – no need for a letter.

I will quickly send you all the articles of your choice by return post, first class.

Clearly, the sooner you get that letter in the post, the quicker you will be able to use some very readable copy at a price you cannot afford to miss out on – <u>nothing.</u>

Yours sincerely

MEL LEWIS

The Financial Services Act now commits us to a more detailed sign-off, which includes the main address and telephone number of Merchant Investors Assurance Company Ltd, which is part of the MI Group, and so on.

'Free' is a powerful word; you can sell almost anything through intelligent price manipulation, and from a buyer's point of view nothing is smarter than zilch! Besides, here was something good being offered for nothing.

In the event, the offer quickly proved irresistible to 50 editors of in-house magazines, including those of Shell, BP, British Sugar, Tate & Lyle, Thomson Holidays, and to 30 editors of newspapers and newspaper groups – the *Yorkshire Evening Post, Western Morning News*, Eastern Daily Press and London Newspaper Group among them.

To date some 70 articles have appeared in the series, with titles such as: 'Why a Man Should Put a Price on the Life of His Wife' (on insuring wives); 'Why Sell Shares When You Can Exchange Them?'; 'The Truth about Timeshare Holiday Homes'; and others more specifically on company products such as 'A New Type of Policy for Those Who Believe in Life Before Death' (protecting against so-called 'dread diseases', where cash is paid out on diagnosis); 'This Way for a Cheaper Pension'; and so on.

Note that the titles are as snappy as any general features title. If the *Daily Mail* uses a lively features format for its financial section every Wednesday, if *The Times* calls its Saturday finance pullout 'Money', you can be sure that rather more downmarket organs, as local and provincial papers tend to be, will also appreciate a light touch, however 'heavy' the topic.

Evening Telegraph, 28 November 1988

No lacklustre pension — if you're careful

by Mel Lewis

NOBODY these days takes the State pension (£41.15 a week for a single person, £65.90 for a married couple) seriously. Or the State Earnings Related Pension Scheme (SERPS), which is linked to salary over a number of years.

Anybody can have a personal pension and now for the first time no employer can lock you into his company's possibly lacklustre pension scheme or insist that you join it as a condition of getting a job.

Also new is the option to stop making payments to SERPS and claw back some of the money paid in to boost your new personal pension.

ALL new-style personal pensions are "portable", so you can take yours with you from job to job. Another feature they have in common is their incredible tax efficiency. All contributions to a pension fund merit tax relief at the highest rate of tax you pay.

So a standard rate taxpayer contributes only £75 for a £100 investment, while a top rate taxpayer needs find only 60p for every £1 of pension. The Government makes up the balance!

The Revenue perks continue. A pension fund grows virtually free of all tax, making savings via a pension plan the most profitable type of saving available to you.

Nevertheless, a personal pension isn't right for everyone. If you are in a good company pension scheme and expect to stay in that job you may be wise to stick with that pension.

According to official figures, only men aged under 43 and women younger than 34 are likely to be better off making personal arrangements for additional pension provision, instead of relying on SERPS.

WHICH pension you choose and how to play your options, depends on your age, the date you fix for retire-

ment, career plans and earnings prospects. It's a big decision and one best taken with expert advice.

You can vary your contributions at any time, a particularly useful safeguard for the self-employed and those who change jobs a lot.

There is built-in protection. If you fall seriously ill and can't keep up the payments they are made for you. MI's Retirement Programme also offers life insurance with the same tax benefits you enjoy on your pension payments, lower terms for non-smokers, and automatic trust facilities, so your family gets all the money you've thoughtfully provided for them, without having to share it with the taxman.

Compiled by Merchant Investors Assurance Company Limited (a member of LAUTRO), which is part of the MI Group. If you'd like to be contacted with full details of the Retirement Programme, please contact Merchant Investors Assurance Company Limited, St. Bartholomew's House, Lewins Mead, Bristol BS1 2NH. (Tel. 0272 250888).

Leicester Mercury, 15 Nov 1988

How to get
a mortgage as
big as the Ritz

Borehamwood Times, 29 Dec 1988

"THE rich are different from us...." F. Scott F. quipped, "Th...

THESE
power and
"Nowadays
tacular. We
matter of ro
manager of t
Harrods Es
prime location
also produce a
does money go
Kevin Ryan
sized Victorian
£760,000 in Janu
for £1.2m.

"We're now se
for £1m each. A
some were only
stopped, Mr Ryan
prices property re
paying more."
Of course it's
"underwriting is str
routine whereby a
cleared by a high-po
back potential of the
So whereas MI
mortgage application
take a few days or w
for a £500,000 loan w
"We look at the in
record of the applicant
Lenders safeguard t
"plenty of equity in th
least". So if the borro
the property needs to b
quick sale, and the
proceeds.
Bob points to the fac
volatile areas of London
in recent months. "It's
Docklands to drop £50,0
shift it. If the borrower ha
lent too much, there could
There was a time wh
penalised for taking large
odds in interest rates. Now
woken up to the fact that
more profit. "We can usu
the rest of the market. Big
record of being able to ha
says.
Because mortgage busine
ness, the Group is rapidly a
major force in the mortgage
appointed to the panel o
Corporation (NHL), a prime
institutions — both Abbey Li
MI Group now also has a
Manhattan, the second largest
to arrange loans of £1 billion th
Bob Warrick says there are
to lessen the repayments burc
your mortgage had become a st
rate rises, consider that somec
mortgage is having to find close
against £750 eight months ago.
There are fixed rate deals ava
low-start scheme which eases th
first few years.
So if you are a ho...
(Mortgage Un...
loan.

How to get a mortgage as big as The Ritz

"THE rich are different from us...." F. Scott Fitzgerald mused to his friend Ernest Hemingway. "Yes," Hemingway quipped, "They have more money!"

These days they also have more borrowing power and the ability to service king-sized mortgages. "Nowadays, a £250,000 home loan is nothing spectacular. We handle mortgages up to £500,000 as a matter of routine," says Bob Warrick, group products manager of the MI Group.

Harrods Estate Agency assures me that big properties in prime locations are always good sellers.

Kevin Ryan of Harrods Estate Agency cited a mansion-sized Victorian town house in Mayfair he had sold for £760,000 in January 1987 and then again in February this year for £1.2 million.

"We're now selling flats in Fountain House on Park Lane for £1 million each. A few years ago when they were refurbished some were only £600,000."

But the upward spiral has stopped, Mr Ryan says.

It's also sometimes slower because expensive property — £1 million and more in London and a good deal less in the country — tends to be unique and to need a rather more thorough survey.

So whereas MI is regularly turning round "normal" mortgage applications on a 24-hour basis, large loans may take a few days or weeks to arrange.

"We look at the integrity, lifestyle, previous borrowing record of the applicant. Usually it's a person of means with an existing substantial property, perhaps a villa abroad, a yacht, that kind of thing," says Bob Warrick.

Even so, at this level lend... themselves comfo... "plenty of ...

... ilat property ...tatile areas of London .cent months. "It's nothing unusual for a seller in Docklands to drop £50,000 on a

Financial advice from Mel Lewis

£600,000 property just to shift it."

There was a time when big borrowers seemed to be penalised for taking large loans by having to pay over the odds in interest rates. That's changed as lenders have woken up to the fact that mammoth mortgages also mean more profit.

The Group is rapidly achieving its goal of becoming a major force in the mortgage market, and has recently been appointed to the panel of the National Home Loans Corporation (NHL), a prime funding source for approved institutions — both Abbey Life and Allied Dunbar failed to get on to the NHL panel.

MI Group now also has a lending facility with Chase Manhattan, the second largest bank in America, and expects to arrange loans of £1bn this year.

Bob Warrick says there are a number of helpful schemes to lessen the repayments burden. Because if you thought your mortgage had become a stinker in the wave of interest rate rises, consider that someone with a typical £100,000 mortgage is having to find close on £1,100 a month gross set against £750 eight months ago.

There are fixed rate deals available for five years, and a low-start scheme which eases the interest payments for the first few years.

So if you are a housebuyer *...* "loadsamoney" MI *...* 250750) is *...* l...

*...*nvestors *...*L), which is part of the MI *...*up. If you'd like to be contacted with full details of the Homeowners Programme, please contact Merchant Investors Assurance Company Limited, St Bartholomew's House, Lewins Mead, Bristol BS1 2NH (Tel: 0272 250888)

Potters Bar Times, Edgware & Mill Hill Times, Barnet Borough Times, 29 December 1988

Figure 2. *I write and syndicate a free financial column on behalf of the MI Group. These are some cuttings from my file. The column goes to 50 editors of house magazines and 30 editors of provincial newspapers – many big names among them. It's a publicity vehicle that also results in a surprising amount of actual business when readers respond to the information and use the phone number featured in the text.*

89

It is encouraging that the *Birmingham Daily News*, which has been taking the series since it began in 1987, and which features items regularly in its Money News section, has just (as I write) been voted Personal Finance Local Newspaper of the Year.

The financial arrangement behind this unusual and effective PR operation is simple. The sponsoring company pays me a fee per article and picks up the distribution tab too. It should be an easy matter to run off 80 identical articles on a set mailing list.

In fact, there are closer to 100, when all the 'internal' courtesy/ information/marketing copies for company managers and directors are taken into account.

My experience says that writers who are any good at writing are best left to get on with writing. Find someone else to handle the drudgery of any kind of mailings, is my advice. All it takes is money.

This isn't the end of the success story, however. You should also monitor any sort of PR campaign. So these sponsored financial pieces are mailed also to two press cuttings bureaux – Durrants and Romeike & Curtice. Why two? It's a failsafe. What the readers of one company fail to spot, the others will pick up, or so the theory goes.

The cuttings (Figure 2) make a meaty contribution to the regular file of company 'mentions' circulated by the MI Marketing Department. Good news for my client, and good news for me too, as everyone who matters sees that Mel is delivering the goods.

Financial services is just one topic with guaranteed reader appeal. There are any number of others. How about estate agents, auction houses, solicitors, dentists, cosmetics and bodycare retailing groups? Might newspapers and magazines not warm to the offer of well-written free articles on topics suggested by the specialisms of these practitioners? All you have to do is find your sponsor. Just hope I don't get there first!

How one man became an expert writer in his own field

Peter Cotterell runs Exhibitor Services ('Making Your Exhibitions Work') and is probably best known for the hard-hitting seminars he runs entitled the Exhibition Goldmine. Peter appreciates the value of a good title as well as anyone, and has recently started his own newsletter, *Exhibition File*, to which I contribute.

Exhibition File isn't an anodyne, 'isn't my company great?' organ, but a regular rabble-rousing blast at an industry that doesn't appreciate what a good thing it's got going for it – exhibitions and trade shows can be a tremendous source of business and great fun too.

So Peter and his contributors regularly sound off about catering and accommodation rip-offs at conference centres and exhibition halls and restrictive practices among the tradespeople whose services are crucial to trade shows. I wrote on how to get better publicity pictures at an exhibition – the *File* is earning a reputation as the *Private Eye* of the exhibitions industry!

Peter doesn't chase personal writing commissions; editors chase him for expert, often anarchic comment on topics relating to exhibitions and conferences. He doesn't plug his own company in every second line or, indeed, at all; his comments carry their own conviction and are, by implication, a far stronger testimonial than any puffery.

If you have some special skill or expert knowledge you too could find yourself in demand as a 'pundit on paper'. Peter is well established and views his writing contributions as an image-enhancing and amusing perk of his profession. As a newcomer, you might assume a more aggressive stance and solicit commissions. After all, nothing ventured, nothing gained. All it takes, as with most things in this life, is an 'acceptable form of words'. You should be confident enough to tackle a suitable letter selling your writing services by the time you reach the end of this book.

Here's how Peter handles himself when an editor calls. 'I have a set charge – £100 per 1000 words. I spend a lot of time researching and writing. If any less is offered, I don't do the job. If I were asked to write on something less familiar to me, say on the increase in Chinese restaurants in Bedfordshire [we were having lunch in one at the time], I would charge £150, which I take to be a top professional rate for 1000 words.'

Evidently, he meets little resistance to his quid pro quo – which in most cases, incidentally, is more than the going rate for trade paper contributions – since editors keep coming back for more. Even 'new' editors say yes to Peter's terms: 'Editors talk to editors. They know how much other editors pay, and therefore how much I charge.'

Some businessmen/writers don't charge at all, of course. This suggests two things to an editor. That the article will be used as a publicity platform for the firm's products or services. Or that the quality of writing will be second-best – after all, nobody knows better than a businessman that you get what you pay for.

Peter sees the market for genuine journalism in trade papers as wide open. 'In the past 10 years the amount of true journalism in trade magazines has been negligible. The papers themselves are often comics, put together by an ad manager and someone who can sub press releases.

'The title might claim sales of 10,000 and a readership of 30,000. In fact the circulation might be 10,000 (not the same as sales) and the true readership 1000, made up of advertisers and their competitors!'

Peter says readers are aware that many trade papers are sycophantic vehicles, and cites the case of a writer friend who wrote a piece slagging off an advertiser just as the editor was attempting to turn the company into a major space-taker. The article was censored and the writer resigned in disgust.

Another time there was an article on how to do better business in Russia: 'It might have been written by *Pravda*. I would have written: "Thirty Things To Be Careful of in Russia." Beware of attractive ladies, there's a lot of entrapment. Beware of changing money, the KGB are on the lookout for people laundering money. Don't be depressed if, after two days of trying to make contacts, you've only met scruffy "messenger boys" without business cards. These are the advance party; they're sussing you out. If you put your pillow over the phone in a hotel, someone will come and tell you the phone's out of order – they're all bugged. And so on.

'*Exhibition File* doesn't take advertising because we want to report accurately. The editor – and the readers – may not agree with what I say, may not like what I say. But the best PR for me, from the point of view of my business, is to be seen as unbiased. The writing is that of an honest broker, pure consultancy.'

For this reason, Peter prefers only the bleakest credit at the foot of the pieces he contributes: 'Peter Cotterell is Secretary General of the National Exhibitors Association. For a free information pack and helpful advice on exhibitions, write to ... [address on page 160].'

'If I tagged on a plug I would lose credibility, dilute all that had gone before. Editors start to trust you. Insert plugs and they use you less and less. However, if I wanted to advertise that would be acceptable. The danger is where the would-be contributor must also be an advertiser or he doesn't get to be a contributor.'

One last tip. Peter often gets his point across by writing letters to the trade papers. As a letter-writer, even a vitriolic and an entertaining one, he's one among many. How does he ensure that his missive enjoys a better-than-average chance of seeing the light of print? 'I keep it short, keep it tight and tell it like it is.'

Targeting PR features

A PR feature is more than just a long press release. It's a complete story that can be run 'as is' in a paper. If you want your copy to stand a fighting chance of being used, it won't carry a product puff in every paragraph. Ideally, it will have wide general interest, unless it is designed to appear, for example, on the motoring or gardening page. It's free, like a press release and differs from the complimentary syndicated articles discussed on page 84 only in that a PR article is an *ad hoc* submission, rather than a regular item.

Within intelligent limits, your press release is mailed to any number of editors, normally in exactly the same form. If their papers happen to have slightly duplicated readership areas, at the borders of a territory where there is often an overlap of circulation, that won't be a problem. Even where a town is served by rival journals you'll mail all the editors involved and lose no sleep over it.

A release, if used at all, may be heavily re-written (or sometimes cut to shreds) by the sub-editors, but an article is different and may well appear unaltered. Which is why care must be taken with targeting if you are to continue to win friends and influence people as a PR.

For instance, you might consider it a great coup to place an article in both the *Manchester Evening News* and the *Liverpool Echo*, until you discover that these have significant circulation overlap. The answer is either to send out dissimilar stories on the same topic, or to mail one paper and only send to the second paper once you've discovered that the first editor is not interested. To maximise your chances of notching up column inches:

- Study the papers you want to hit. Get the ad manager to send you sample back issues. He will, once you convince him you're a potential advertiser.
- Turn an editor into a friend. How? Give him a ring when he's done you a good turn and used your material. Say thanks. Then find out what he wants to see and send more of it. Short of this personal touch, enclose a card which asks: Did you like the piece? Will you use it? Would you like more? What is interesting to your readership?
- Cultivate a local stringer, preferably a photojournalist. If your client is staging a competition to promote his goods, get the stringer to interview a local winner. Regional press launches of products or services are another smart move that will boost your chances of winning press mentions. Make sure local shops are stocked with the goods, though!
- Include a picture to boost your success rate dramatically.
- Freesheets are a howling success, in spite of early resistance from readers and advertisers alike. They are also more receptive to press material because they are more mindful of their costs than the paid-for papers and grateful for the free help your copy represents.

How to ensure the best possible publicity photographs

Your photographs, like your copy, should be good enough for the purpose for which they are meant. Use a professional photographer if you have the money and cultivate a responsive photographer, when you find one, so that he or she comes to understand what you require in your shots. Otherwise, learn how to take adequate pictures yourself – or get a colleague to master the skills.

It isn't as easy as the books tell you, and the latest autofocus hocus-pocus space probe lookalike will not necessarily turn you into a David Bailey. In fact, autofocus can be a pain rather than a blessing. Aim the camera at a group of people and the gadget may 'miss' the heads, if no head is dead centre of your group, and focus on the distant background, so blurring the faces you're trying to record.

You don't need ace equipment, but it helps from the image point of view. It's hard to imagine that a salesman who drives up in a Roller is anything other than good at selling. In the same way, good gear suggests you know what you're doing as a photographer, and people respond accordingly. Your subjects are more inclined to take you seriously, and anyone who has ever toted a professional-looking camera outfit will know that it opens doors wonderfully.

There are also some good practical reasons for choosing reasonably sophisticated equipment. A motor drive is a boon. It lets you catch many more shots than winding film on manually. And there's something else that I've never seen mentioned in any book on photography.

It always puzzled me that camera designers had opted to place the viewfinder on SLR cameras centrally, and the wind-on lever close to it, on the right. This meant that I would take a shot and then have to move the camera away from my head in order to wind on comfortably without bashing my fingers into my face.

One day the penny dropped. Most people are 'right-eyed'. Sighting via the right eye, it's easy enough to flick the wind-on lever and keep the camera pressed against your nose, still monitoring the scene, ready for the next shot. I happen to be left-eyed. There must be others like me. The simple solution is to use a motor drive.

A selection of lenses is a must, not for the kudos but because they give you, quite literally, a fresh perspective on a scene. I work with a 180mm F2.8, a 50mm F1.2, and a 20mm F2.8 on a Nikon FE2 camera. I prefer the middle lens for portrait work, even though it does take in more than just a 'head and tie'; it's faster (enables me to take good shots without flash even in poor light) than most portrait lenses, and is a good compromise when you suddenly have to include more than a face and don't want to be bothered with changing lens in mid-session.

I use a Metz flash with a special module that clips on to the camera shoe and lets me take advantage of the TTL (Through The Lens) metering system on the FE2, which automatically adjusts the amount of flashlight being emitted. It's near-on 100 per cent reliable.

The point is that you must be comfortable with your camera, and that means practice, not on assignments, but in a controlled setting, where you can try different aperture and speed settings and monitor the results (see Figure 3).

I've spent a lot of time studying photography, and I still find it hard to 'keep in trim'; I simply don't take enough pictures from day to day to be mindful constantly of all the facets of taking a good publicity picture. One thing worth remembering: unlike writing, which is a 'make and mend' activity, photography is a 'nervy' occupation demanding total concentration, therefore you should never drink while taking pictures. It's a lethal combination.

For all these reasons, it pays to take plenty of shots and also to 'bracket' them, if you have time. This is a common technique when shooting in colour, using film which will turn into slides. You set what you take to be the optimum reading and take a shot. Then you open up the 'eye' of the lens (the aperture) to let in more light and take a shot, and also close it down for a third shot with less light reaching the film. So if you take a picture at F5.6, you would also shoot at F8 (letting in half as much light) and F4 (letting in twice as much light). Most of the time, however, you will be shooting in black-and-white film (I prefer Kodak TMax 400, which is fast enough even for poor light conditions) and your finished prints will ideally be 10 × 8in single-weight glossies, in studio jargon.

Shots for record purposes, such as a view of your client's stand at an exhibition, should be in black and white *and* colour. Colour work is more informative. At a pinch, though, settle for colour prints, not transparencies or slides. The negatives from which colour prints are made also reproduce in black and white with minimal loss of definition.

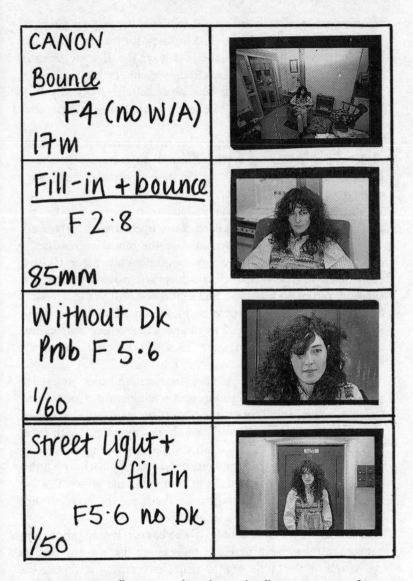

Figure 3. *It will pay you to learn how to handle a camera, even if you never become a full-blown photojournalist (see page 94). The way to do this, to be comfortable with your camera and make fewer mistakes, is to practise taking shots in a controlled setting, where you can try different aperture settings, test your flashgun etc. Later you can study the results.*

Amateurs frequently stand too far away from their subjects. Always take a step forward before pressing the button, there may be a better shot two feet nearer. I always feel slightly criminal about chopping off people's legs in the viewfinder, but the truth is papers are only interested in head and shoulder shots as a rule. Waste film with unwanted 'bits' and you are losing definition for the faces that really matter.

Never be afraid to pose people. The more positive you are about manoeuvring them, the better. If people suspect you may be an amateur they'll voice their irritation and further erode your courage.

Whatever type of photograph you're taking, if it's for the press, it will look better against a plain, uncluttered – best of all, white or pale grey – background. For the model-in-a-planter's-chair shot on page 73 we used a roll of studio white paper. Cloth is more prone to creasing and the shadows will mar your picture. If shooting out of doors, try to find a stuccoed wall to use as a backdrop. At a pinch set your subjects against something without prominent outlines, as far away from any actual objects as you can, and then open up the aperture as far as is practicable, to put the background out of focus.

Shots taken with flash can look unnaturally harsh, unless the flash can be bounced off a ceiling, wall or white card. Shadows can be lightened by standing people well away from walls. Much of the time, of course, you will be combining flashlight with other background light, natural or otherwise. If shooting in colour, watch for mixed colour 'temperatures', especially with strip lighting. This can give a reddish light or a cold blue glow. The eye rationalises mixed-up lighting so we don't see the problem, but your camera will record the scene faithfully.

A consistent warm or cold 'cast' can be corrected in processing; a mixed cast may be incurable. Simply check that the numbers on the barrels of neon tubes are the same, and turn off or replace the odd ones out. Where success is critical, take Polaroid shots to preview each picture and check the colour balance and composition.

Which type of view is best: landscape or portrait? Where cost permits, send editors a selection with your press release; or take a landscape shot that can be cropped to fit a single column slot on the page, even if that means turning a crowd scene into a close-up of your client holding his latest widget.

As for portraits, people look best if they stand with their shoulders turned obliquely to the photographer, but with their head looking almost square at the camera. Editors like to have faces turning into the page, so give a choice of right- or left-handed pose – everything to maximise your chances of getting into print and winning publicity.

Keep a file of pictures, cuttings from magazines etc, that you think work. Ask yourself how the photographer achieved his effect; talk to professionals and ask their advice; read loads of books on beginning photography and cross-reference the different points in your head, never mind notes. If several authors say the same thing, it may well be right.

Another tip: read 'little' books for close-focus information on one particular aspect of photography. Focal Press did a whole series of books on available light photography, photographing animals, machinery, and what have you. Such books are far better than the coffee table style of handbook, larded with pin-ups and colour views, that tries to tackle every aspect of this huge subject. Keep your eyes open when you do the rounds of second-hand bookshops: the Focal Press books went out of print several decades ago.

Case history 1

Having written a 9000 word brochure on the mortgage service offered by one of the country's biggest insurance companies, my problem then was how to distribute the brochures aggressively, rather than simply wait for customers to pick them up casually from a pile in the company's offices.

All the traditional marketing routes lay open to me; mail out the brochure with a press release; offer use of the copy in the brochure free to the press, if the company's name was credited with providing the information; throw a press reception, and concoct a press kit with the brochure included, and so on.

All these methods, being tried and tested, work. But they are all *boring*. And one thing the publicist is constantly having to do, as you must learn if you wish to promote your own business and understand publicity, is *cross the boredom threshold*.

The mortgage brochure marketing problem was particularly tricky. The financial press are interested in the subject, obviously, and the topic has become more newsworthy these past years, thanks to the important property market. Nevertheless, a mortgage brochure is one among many, and never mind that mine was longer and more informative than many.

Now it happened that a conference on the mortgage market was about to take place; however, the company for whom I had written the brochure was not involved with this event. Clearly, the organisers would be doing their own promotional press mailings, so why not, I suggested to my insurance company client, either *get* involved with the conference and 'piggy back' their mailings, or simply announce the conference in our own press release, and enclose our mortgage brochure with this 'pirate' announcement. The point is that a conference is pegged to a date, and is therefore newsworthy. A brochure, being timeless, lacks urgency in the eyes of a newsman. Put the two together, and something of the razzamatazz of the live show might rub off on our publication.

Case history 2

I was working for an insurance broking group who were covering the high-risk life of stuntman Dave Gauder. Gauder had lined up a number of spectacular record attempts over the summer months. The first was to lift a Metro van at the British Truck Grand Prix at Silverstone; next he was to be roped to two high-revving speedboats in London's Docklands, the location of the International Powerboat Grand Prix, in a bid to stop the boats speeding off and taking his arms with them! Then there was talk of holding down a helicopter trying to take off and towing Concorde. It was, after all, the silly season.

Silverstone was something of a washout. Gauder failed to lift the Metro – he merely raised it, but still earned a second *Guinness Book of Records* mention. I had invited all the London and national and Sunday picture and news editors to send photographers and reporters, as well as the Birmingham (Gauder is a Brummy) and national TV stations.

The point about press releases is you have to keep your eye on the ball. The chances of the papers mentioning the name of my client – the Porchester Group, whose name was emblazoned on stuntman Gauder's T-shirt – was remote. The best that could be expected was a good clear photograph of the company's name on Gauder's chest – which is why television is so potent a medium for sponsorship campaigns. Radio was irrelevant, therefore, and I judged that the motoring publications would be out in force anyway, so no prompting was needed from me.

The Docklands stunt was a success, with Dave breaking three world records, and I ignored the boating press for similar reasons. Then Gauder arranged a second crack at the Metro, on the occasion of the opening of Birmingham's first-ever Fitness Show at the National Exhibition Centre. I went back to the original target audience for the third time.

These editors were being mailed by name, and by now they would have picked up some of the excitement of the challenge. In addition, there was also human interest kindling in the man's determination in the face of adversity, as well as the sheer grit and brute strength needed to lift a van weighing 2000lb! The fitness and health efficiency magazines were also ignored – they'd be there anyway.

Through all these events, we had held off announcing any of the stunts, or the involvement of my client, to one of the most important markets for the Group, the insurance trade papers (*Money Marketing, Prospect*, and so on), partly because they were unlikely to bother with the expensive business of sending a photographer; and partly because my client wanted above all a story of success, not just the fairly trivial information that they were insuring a high-risk life.

So I resuméd all three releases into one, to make a fourth, and attached a photograph of the stuntman in a Herculean pose, harnessed to the Metro. Four releases, one a week; it *can* be done, if there is a running theme to sustain interest, and if the news content is lively enough in itself.

The Concorde stunt was also successfully accomplished and pictures of Gauder, emblazoned with my client's name and tugging Concorde across the tarmac, appeared in virtually every national daily paper.

7
How to Devise and Implement a Marketing Method

How do I – how can you – get writing work, whether in PR or journalism? Let me take PR first, it's a shorter story.

I let people know I'm around and I ask for what I want. When I bought a house in a small town in Norfolk I discovered the offices of a lively ad agency round the corner in a converted house. I mailed the MD (by name) with a letter, a self-publicity leaflet and a few choice cuttings. We talked and I wrote some brochure and sales letter copy for the agency, which then grew and upped and moved to a larger town miles away. Such is life!

My propositioning letter went like this:

Dear . . .

You'll remember: I came in a few days back to use your fax machine. Thanks for staying with it when the wires weren't right first time round. But something else.

Your outfit seemed pretty busy when I dropped in and I suspect it was no accident that it looked that way. It occurs to me you might need copywriting/editing help from time to time and I should take this opportunity to point out that I now have a base a few hundred yards away at . . . , as well as the London address above.

I work in financial services, antiques and fine art, hi-tech, ghost writing for MDs, magazine production from start to finish (barring design), all else you see on the enclosed self-publicity sheet, and you name it.

If I'm saying anything that interests you and you want to talk, give me a ring. And if not, I'll still be pleased to use and pay for your fax facility.

Yours sincerely

MEL LEWIS

Short, friendly, a handshake and a sales pitch all in one. Sometimes I try harder.

One company whose publicity I receive is forever breaking the rule that says you don't blow your own trumpet, but instead talk about what you can do for the client. This company constantly tells potential clients, via ads, salesletters and a newsletter, how wonderful and successful it has been. Most irritating of all, it's true: last year they pulled in 42 new clients!

Obviously, they're doing something right. But I know that they are not doing their newsletter right. Newsletters normally enjoy a poor readership, largely because usually they rattle on about the companies whose publicity vehicles the rags are. I say there's a better way to do it. It's easy to understand but hard to put into practice.

You put the reader and his interests first. This means that titbits of news and gossip about staff and their charity matches and extramural achievements take a back seat to items of burning importance to the readers – namely how to do more and better business.

I used to do the newsletter for PNA. The lead stories of two issues were headed like this:

THE PNA WAY TO MAKE
THE MOST OF YOUR POST

The other said:

REMARKABLE NEW SYSTEM HELPS BUSY
PRs DO MORE AND BETTER BUSINESS

Some years ago I wrote to the MD of the first company which constantly trumpets its achievements. I pitched for business and got a bullish letter back, the gist of which was thanks, but no thanks. When I got another rah, rah letter a few weeks back, I knocked on his door again.

Dear Mr ...

Thank you for your letter of .... . I'd like to write copy for ... [name of the newsletter], and I'll tell you why.

I've watched your company grow. Your ambition is well focused, the approach bullish. You are obviously doing a lot right. But not ... [newsletter].

People who read your journal are a lot less interested in your successes than in what you can do for them. It takes a special eye to write 'you' copy and find stories that intrigue readers, rather than tickle the self-esteem of the sponsoring company.

You're doing well. I say you could do even better – particularly on this front. I know you're a hard nut to crack. But if you understand what I'm saying, how can you ignore my message?

Yours sincerely

MEL LEWIS

I received a bright, thumbs down letter in reply. Will I keep knocking (perhaps kicking is closer to it) at this door? Why not? Remember that old Chinese proverb about the stone and dripping water. Where you have some special qualification for talking to people and getting work, use it. I sent this letter to every major organiser of antique fairs:

HOW TO BECOME A WEALTHIER FAIRS ORGANISER IN 1988

You've known me for the past five years as the fairs columnist of *Antique Dealer and Collector's Guide*. From early in the new year that association is to end.

Amicably, in fact. But as you can see from the enclosed publicity which I wrote for *Writing to Win*, my new book, other more businesslike activities beckon.

I've enjoyed working with you for the fairs page. But actually I am hoping that now we will have even more to do with each other . . . I guarantee it will be to your advantage.

Let me explain. I've seen the best publicity fairs organisers have to offer. And I've seen the rest. If you handle your own publicity, you probably shouldn't. You should leave it to a professional. And if you thought you'd been doing that, well all I can say is you have not been very well served.

The trouble is, people who haven't seen first-rate publicity don't know what to expect. So they accept what they're given, and the meagre results achieved. More importantly, people who work with amateurs – even enthusiastic ones – will never appreciate what a professional can achieve.

When I wrote a press release for the London Antique Dealers Fair, I turned organiser Jane Sumner into a national celebrity overnight. The fair was written up in *The Times*, the *Daily Telegraph*, while the *London Evening Standard* devoted half a page to a story based on the release.

In addition, Jane was on the radio on numerous occasions, talking about the haunted chair I'd written up. Have you any idea what that type of publicity is worth . . . what it would cost if you had to pay for that amount of advertising space and air time?

I also number among my clients Cumpers and Martin Dodge, both fine reproduction furniture manufacturers, as well as Dragons of Walton Street, who recreate elegant painted furniture based on traditional designs.

As I say, you deserve a better service – the best. Why not start the new year working with a seasoned professional who understands the business, and also appreciates what you are trying to achieve, and who knows how to get results – not only in the trade papers, but also in the national Press?

The first thing you will discover is that the price of such a service is far more comfortable than you would ever have thought.

With best wishes for a prosperous new year!

Yours sincerely

Mel Lewis

MEL LEWIS

Out of about 20 people mailed I picked up four new clients – a howling success, in other words. The only better way I've come across of finding new clients is via writing books. Satisfied readers have been turning into hot prospects. They must have been working with deadwood, and my enthusiasm seems to be a great recommendation. The good news is that they come to me, out of the blue.

Editors are different, on balance a much more dour breed than business people – another good reason to keep irons in both fires. They are a harder pitch. You will need to be tenacious, prolific and understanding about their needs.

I have worked out a format for a sales letter and a monitoring and follow-up system (more of which later) which benefit from being simple and effective.

A letter – any sort of letter – starts with a piece of paper. Every serious writing contender needs a letterhead. Without launching into a treatise on letterheads, let me make a couple of points that I hope will make the penny drop.

In almost any transaction you need to establish credentials. Yet at the same time, good manners, the Christian ethic, or something, dictates that we don't make a song and dance about our achievements. Listing my previous writing posts, books, and so on, on my letterhead, in print, gets round this problem. The editor sees what I've done, but I haven't boasted about it in the text.

Do editors find this type of letterhead pushy, over the top? Very, very few, as far as I can judge. In one case I applied for a writing job on a magazine and the editor wrote back to say the job

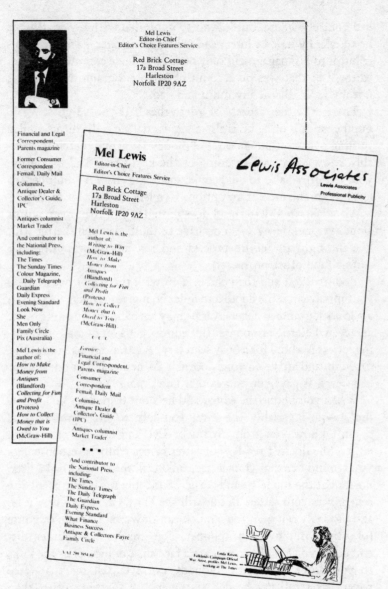

Figure 4. *Your letterhead is your calling card and statement of credentials all in one. Using a photograph or an image personalises your paper. My letterhead features a drawing of me working at* The Times *by Linda Kitson, 'Falklands Campaign Official War Artist'. An illustrated letterhead also ensures other less obvious benefits. See page 108.*

had gone elsewhere, but he was so impressed with my credentials he asked if I would be interested in being a stringer – a regular contributor to his magazine. I only once got a snide comment from an editor, but that was on account of my photograph. Now that's not my fault. Blame my mum and dad.

There are other aspects of a letterhead. If you've got a VAT number stick it on. This is also a 'credential': it tells editors you're turning over a serious amount of money a year and therefore probably know what you're doing at the keyboard. And if you use your letterhead also to bill people, including the VAT number is a legal requirement, not an option. I've left the best bit to last.

An 'illustrated' letterhead does more for you than mere words alone ever can. How so? You have to think through (better still, live through) the entire process and rhythm of propositioning editors (and other prospects).

You mail out and then chase. You wish the editor had studied your missive in some depth and quickly, but reality says that it's in a pile with umpteen others. Or he may have made some note on it, and even dictated a response. But editors get a lot of mail and finding letters is a bind for a busy secretary. A letter can take days to be typed up and arrive on your doormat. Whether it's good news or bad news, it pays you to get that news quickly.

When you phone the editor and he's out or tied up 'in a meeting', as is invariably the case, you talk to his secretary. She doesn't know you from Adam or Eve and doesn't care much either. She doesn't recall your letter or the editor's response *until* you remind her that your letter, unlike all the others, had a little portrait at the top left-hand corner. Suddenly she is animated! She remembers your letter. Better still she knows exactly where it is, and probably can give you a quick run-down on the ed's response (or otherwise) over the phone. You aren't just another disembodied voice, either. You are a face she can look at as she talks to you down the wires. Nobody can ever tell me that 'face paper', as I call my headed stationery, is anything other than good news to a writer.

If the ed isn't interested in your suggestion, you can quickly get on with propositioning the next editor on your hit list.

I say most business letters benefit from a heading, but those that go to editors more than most. Editors eat, drink and breathe titles, headlines. They will also respond to yours, if they're any good.

Also, of course, if they're relevant. Editors (and people generally) are busy. They'll give you a few seconds of their time, and then that's it. What they're saying is 'interest me . . . give me a reason for going on and reading your letter.' The title you use doesn't have to be a headline in the accepted sense (see Chapter 4), nor do you have to use the same title on the article offered when you submit it, though it will pay you to remind the editor of the title on the letter that won the commission, because it's all part of a continuing process. If something works, stick with it.

The three examples that follow show just how easy it is to pen a lively propositioning letter to an editor:

SECRETS OF THE SNAPPING PROFESSIONALS

Not another idea for an article on top pros, with their hints and tips for better photographs. But solid advice from those whose jobs demand that they take good, usable shots day in, day out.

People who may know little about photography. Or even care. Yet still they have to produce the goods.

I'm talking about snapshooting:

ESTATE AGENTS . . . picking flattering angles against the odds.
SURVEYORS . . . monitoring rot, subsidence.
AUCTIONEERS, ANTIQUE DEALERS . . . keeping track of goods for catalogues, records, security.
MOTOR MART MAGAZINES . . . who offer free photos with ads.

At Grosvenor House Antiques Fair, glossiest in the calendar, I caught the organiser doing the rounds with his 'idiot-proof' Konica flash outfit.

'The roof's leaking,' he revealed. 'I need pictures to show the insurers.'

Recently I talked to Roddy Llewellyn, an accomplished

landscape gardener. He records his work with a lowly Praktica.

My latest assignment has been snapping pieces of antique pine furniture for Miller's Price Guide. Sixty items a day type of thing.

I work with a Leica M4-P, Braun 400M Logic flash and fitted Braun board reflector – virtually a portable ceiling!

It's an interesting, varied story. With a wealth of tips for the photographer concerned more with craft than art.

Let me know your interest.

Sincerely

MEL LEWIS

PS. Samples of the work of these casual cameramen to be included.

'BOB FREQUENTLY LECTURES ON FAIR-GROUND CHILDREN'S EDUCATION'

This intriguing news cutting is from World's Fair, the trade paper for fairs people.

Bob – Robert Pullin – comes from a family of 'travellers'. So he knows first hand about life on the road. He'd be an ideal guide to that curious, closed world.

My suggested article would reveal...How parents and children handle the demands of their roving existence... How well such children learn... What they learn... What opportunities there are to 'escape' the itinerant life.

Perhaps ordinary parents can learn something from these freewheeling children's unusual education.

It promises to be a lively, topical story, with strong picture potential. Let me know your interest.

Yours sincerely

MEL LEWIS

HAS FLUORIDE FAILED?

The *British Dental Journal* reports a type of decay that has only become possible thanks to fluoride.

Basically, there are three layers to a tooth: enamel, dentine and soft pulp. Fluoride toughens enamel. But does nothing to dentine.

Now dentists are seeing that decay can spread through microscopic clefts in the fluoride-toughened enamel.

Caries form in the dentine. And the super-sensitive pulp (resting on the nerve) is also attacked.

So what looks like a perfectly normal, healthy tooth, with a shiny, hard enamel jacket, may in fact have deep-seated rot below the surface.

The trouble is harder to spot. And curing the problem is harder, too, at the dentine level.

Fluoride may be a blessing. But it has also turned out to be a danger in disguise.

Let me know your interest.

Yours sincerely

MEL LEWIS

Dare you send the same idea to several editors at once?

Countless books on writing tell you never to submit the same article idea to more than one editor at a time. Why? Because you risk alienating the editor if it should ever be discovered that you didn't offer him or her an exclusive? Because both editors might come zapping back and commission the 'same' piece?

Or is it just ungentlemanly conduct and offends against some unwritten code of fair play among professionals?

I'll tell you where I stand and you can make your own decisions. If you think editors talk among themselves about ideas you submit, you probably have an inflated idea of the importance of yourself or your work. I don't think editors have ever come back wanting the same piece. But if they ever do, lucky you! You can turn one editor down. You'll feel great doing it, as they'll do it to you often enough.

More likely, you'll find a way to write something on the topic for both journals, and you'll work hard to see that you cover totally different angles for each editor.

As for ethical considerations, it's a jungle out there. If you hold your breath waiting for editors to come back to you within a reasonable time in response to your ideas, even assuming they like and want to use them, you will die in mid-assignment: your first. If you want to stay alive and remain in business, play the field.

I usually work out a hit list of five likely publications. I send each editor the same idea – in a personalised letter, of course. I note these recipients on the simple grid system you see in Figure 5 with the name of the editor, publication, address, phone number, date, title of article idea, and so on. I chase for news of progress on these after a couple of days or a week at most, starting (obviously) with the editor of the publication I would most like to see my work in.

I never send out finished articles. Not even in the rare case where I have written something and had it rejected and the article is ready to go. Either the editor will suspect, accurately, that it's been rejected by another editor, or he'll conclude that you are unbusinesslike enough to write stories without first getting commissions. You will nosedive in his estimation on either count.

ARTICLE: FAIRGROUND CHILDRENS EDUCATION

SENT TO	WHEN	PAPER, ADDRESS	WHEN	RESULT
JOYCE HOPKIRK	28/6 '88	EDITOR, LOOK, SUNDAY TIMES	2/7 '88	SUGGESTS PEOPLE PAGES OR COLOUR MAG
ALISON	28/6 '88	PARENTS		
JANE McLOUGHLIN	28/6 '88	GUARDIAN WOMEN		X POST TO PAY
CATHERINE HADLEY	28/6 '88	EXPRESS WOMEN(?) D. EXPRESS	6/7	NO. Try in future Jill Guyke, Assist. Ed

ARTICLE: SECRETS OF THE JOBBING PROFESSIONALS.

SENT TO	WHEN	PAPER, ADDRESS	PHONE	RESULT
THE ED	17/7 '88	AMATEUR PHOTOGRAPHER	637 942	Tom (Aug '88)
THE ED	"	CAMERA CHOICE	643 8042	No freelance Submission!
THE ED	"	CAMERA WEEKLY	977 8787	Tim (Aug '88)

ARTICLE: FLOURIDE

SENT TO	WHEN	PAPER, ADDRESS	WHEN	RESULTS
ALISON	28/7 '88	PARENTS		

Figure 5. *When submitting article ideas I work out a hit list of five or so likely publications – prime editor targets in other words. This simple grid system helps me keep track of who got what, when, and how the editors reacted to the ideas. The grid goes into an A4 clear plastic wallet, with a copy of my 'sales' letter, correspondence from the editor and initial research material. Should you ever mail the same idea to several editors at the same time? See page 112.*

Write up your article in a sales letter all over again. The editor will think he's seeing something fresh and original. He'll put a bit of his own personality into the article, if it's approved, and you will be able to do a quick re-write of the rejected piece and be quids in. Why 'quids in'? Because you will have been paid by the first editor. Never write anything for nothing – see Chapter 8 for more on this life or death tack.

How to turn one idea into two or more articles

Editors obey all the usual client rules. Give them what they want and what they believe you can reliably supply, but ring the changes. For *Money Mail*, for instance, I wrote 'The Lost Art of Saying Thanks', a piece on tipping in restaurants. Six years later, in 1981, when restaurants were in dire straits, more concerned with where the next customer was coming from, never mind the size of the tip, the editor was pleased to commission a piece called 'Eat, Drink and . . . Be Wary.'

> As they reel from the recession, restaurateurs have come up with some neat, under-the-table ways of picking up extra pounds and pence from unsuspecting customers.
>
> Fiddled cash is quick, easy, and often untaxable. More than ever I find I'm being given the wrong change in restaurants and pubs. Or charged over the odds on a bill.

Latch on to a topic, and then do it to death. I wrote on au pairs for the London *Evening News* and on nannies twice for the Femail pages of the *Daily Mail*. All you have to do is find an angle – give a story an unusual twist, in lay parlance. I did this with: 'How You English Spoil Your Children', in which I gave au pairs a rare opportunity to comment on how we bring up our children.

When my sister's friend discovered the gentle enthusiasm and willingness to work of Japanese au pairs, I wrote about the new oriental wonder: A Bright Answer to Every Woman's Au Pair Dream. And when it was the turn of myself and my partner to hire a nanny, or rather a succession of nannies, to care for our baby boy, in the wake of an ad that drew 140 replies, the article that followed went under the heading: 'The Good Nanny Guide'.

For the nudie magazine *Parade* I wrote 'How Not to Look Like a Married Man'. For the woman's page of the *Daily Express* I switched camps, turned informer and submitted 'How to Spot a Married Man on the Make'. It's a devil of a job being a freelance writer. But the more of a devil you are, the better.

Syndication: the easiest money you'll ever earn from writing

By the early 1970s I had become a prolific writer on the 'new' antiques. Encouraged by David Moss, editor of *Art & Antiques Weekly*, I contributed articles on paper knives (written around my own unique collection), bells, typewriters, picture frames, collectables of the Wild West, guitars, display cases, and more. I'd picked up contracts for two books, one on bottles (then the latest collecting craze) and the other a general collecting book.

In a tiny way I started to experiment with syndication, using this stock of feature material. Syndication is nothing more than a marketing device to sell the same article over and over again, capitalising on the fact that publications often have quite clearly defined circulation areas, and therefore editors are relaxed about accepting previously published pieces, provided they have not been seen in their own circulation areas. In the real world, there is often some overlap of readership areas, and it pays to know the danger spots and keep well clear. I have more to say on circulation later.

There are, of course, other attractive reasons for an editor saying 'yes' to syndicated manuscripts. They tend to be much cheaper, since the author expects to get paid from many sources. The articles are 'tried and tested'. If they have been published, they can't be that bad, and that can be a plus: even the most confident editor is afraid of making mistakes. Then there is always uncertainty in commissioning original material. Will the writer be able to keep up the flow or the quality? With syndicated pieces, the work is already done and immediately available. On three occasions I sold batches of 50, yes 50, articles to one editor, to use as and when he pleased. They were a bargain – for him – and money found for me!

Something else to bear in mind, regarding the psychology of the editor. As a general rule, editors do not get, nor do they solicit, much feedback from their readers. They know when the whole package of goodies – the newspaper – is succeeding from the number of copies sold. But little may be known about the popularity or otherwise of specific columns or articles.

That said, they do get letters from readers, complimentary ones among them, though nothing that a statistician would take to be a representative sample based on sales or readership. What is remarkable is the curious knee-jerk reaction editors exhibit when readers don't like something; so much so that one unfavourable letter can eclipse all the nice ones.

This phenomenon is well known, and mightily feared, among mail order advertisers. One irate customer writing to an editor, complaining about a product bought off the page of that editor's paper, can call into question the entire future of the advertiser involved with that particular journal, even though the advertiser may have spent thousands of pounds in ads and the reader's belly-ache amounts to a few pounds or pence!

The moral is to avoid even the possibility of adverse reader response, such as can come from the same article appearing in two newspapers selling in adjacent areas. Another tip to take from mail order boys: never 'sit' on readers' correspondence, however busy you may be.

Readers occasionally write to the author of an article by name, courtesy of the paper's address. Whatever the question or point, reply immediately and politely, and make sure the reply goes out first-class post, regardless of the stamp or lack of stamp on any reply envelope. Never let a reader run to an editor because you have been slow in replying. Where a distressed reader is involved, every editor turns into a white knight and may even end your writing career on his paper, out of some bizarre professional sense of justice.

Getting started in syndication

To maximise your selling potential you should target newspapers with relatively small and clearly defined circulation areas. Thus, you could land a regular slot with the London evening newspaper, but at a stroke you put out of court all the hundreds of local, mainly weekly, metropolitan papers, as the *London Evening Standard* sells all over London and in fact right across a great swathe of commuter-land, as far north as Bedfordshire and close to the South Coast. By the same token, obviously, you can proposition no national papers as these, by definition, cover the country.

Like all rules, however, this one is dying to be broken. Syndica-tion is about writing is all about making money, and if I were able to land a big-paying slot in a London or a national paper, well, of course, I'd gladly give up all the meaner paying minnows, wouldn't I? No, I wouldn't – nor should you. You simply write on another topic for the big paper, or write on the same topic for both provin-cials and national paper, but ensure that the two versions are as chalk and cheese.

My first syndicating efforts were modest: just a query letter, my credentials for writing antiques articles, a list of titles, a price list, a sample article or two, a reply sheet, a stamped addressed envelope. When I say modest, I mean relatively cheap and quick to organise, and nothing that couldn't be run together in an instant print shop. All these elements of a mail order package are essential.

This was, in effect, a low-cost test mailing, the classic way to handle any new mail order business, and one of the great bonuses of writing from a business viewpoint.

You don't have to spend £40,000 on a shop lease, refurbishing and stocking it, and maybe going down the pan if you mistake your market. The writer can chance his arm with syndication for a few hundred pounds or less. Although when you get going it feels that your only cost is photocopying or printing out pieces of paper, your real ongoing operating costs are not inconsequential and should be quantified and studied. The cost breaks down like this:

Mailing list purchase
List vetting time
Creative time – drafting the selling copy, devising mailing pack
Printing/photocopying
Design (if bought in)

Stationery (envelopes etc)
Postage
Collating/stuffing time
Phone calls
'Chasing' time

Note that I include all the personal time elements. As writers we are encouraged, by editors who commission our work and by the romantic public who read the stuff, to view writing time as elastic and disposable. I dismiss the notion in the face of reality.

Reality presents me with serious and continuing bills to pay, and also with the fair probability that well-directed efforts will result in paying writing work, sometimes handsomely paying work. Speculating with time, therefore, is akin to gambling with actual money.

Now my father was a professor of gambling, so knowledgeable about form that horse and dog trainers came from afar to consult him. Dad also turned out to be a genius at losing money and squandering health, and I was turned off gambling at an early age. But it is, as they say, 'in the blood', so I try to stick to loaded dice and run only with propositions, writing and otherwise, that offer a 60/40 or better chance of success.

Well-written, properly prepared, intelligently targeted syndication falls into the category of a 60/40 shot. Writing a novel does not. My copywriting guru, Lou de Swart, always maintained that he could write a very good novel if someone gave him £10,000 to do it. I'm sure he was right. Only no one ever made him the offer. But that's another story, and I don't say this is a perfect system for all life's decisions and hazards.

Costing out all the time involved in work such as syndication is an intelligent, businesslike thing to do. Not so that you can home in like a laser beam only on writing activities which produce guaranteed big bucks – you may not find any. But so that at some point you can streamline your successful activities and delete some of the drudgery involved.

Hark back to the costing list; you'll see what I mean. Creating a mailing list takes time and effort. Is there a way of cutting corners? Yes. You can buy a list of members of the British Association of

Industrial Editors in the form of sticky, addressed labels. The BAIE list costs £215 plus VAT; see Useful Addresses, page 160. BAIE members (the author among them) are industry communicators, and many edit or help to edit company magazines.

Contrary to popular belief, these in-house magazines do take contributions from outsiders, and they pay sometimes at least as well as local papers. There is another advantage. House magazines have the circulation equivalent of a closed circuit TV audience. For example, I supplied articles to an STC magazine based in Greenwich, south London. People who worked at that depot no doubt commuted from all over London. Very likely the articles I sold to STC appeared, on rare occasions, in identical form in papers local to these workers' homes, because I had sold the editors the same stories. I never had a complaint. In this case, clearly, the medium masks the message.

There are many other list purveyors and brokers. PNA, the media distribution specialist, keeps an up-to-date directory of media personnel, including editors, features editors, news editors, and so on, all available via computer links to your own desk or in hard-copy form as a chunky publication called PNA *Media Guide*. The latter is published every two months. Subscriptions are £150 a year, £50 for a single copy. The price of the computer link, known as PNA Targeter, is available on request (01-377 2521).

The most tedious part of syndication has to be 'stuffing'. At one time I was having to collate and insert nine different slips of paper, bearing lists of articles and various sales blurbs, into packages to go to 500 editors. As I was billing my own time out at £20-£30 an hour at that point, and there was a lively call on it, I decided to take on someone from Gentle Giant, a tackle-anything-no-job-too-small London-based agency, at £11 an hour. Apart from the 'wall of sound' pop music he delighted in working to, the exercise was a success.

One word of warning. Stuffing is so boring it is impossible to maintain concentration. Always random check the contents of the envelopes from time to time, as a means of quality control. I promise you will find mistakes, even if you handle the whole operation yourself.

Stamping hundreds of envelopes, without a franking machine,

is a pain. Until you discover that the Post Office (main branches only) will accept 125 (minimum) same weight envelopes (tied in bundles of 50) for franking. You just pay the bill up front (get a receipt for your tax file) and avoid such transactions in the PO's busy periods.

What are best-selling topics for syndicated articles?

You can't syndicate every subject with equal success. Newsy pieces will obviously date, and although the USA supports the syndicated columns of a lot of very successful news commentators, news is as yet a virtually untapped lode over here. The problem, communication, is close to being solved. The post is obviously too slow and unreliable for news commentary, but electronic mail, which can send a message down the phone wires via your computer, is available, but not yet as accessible to editors as it no doubt will be in years to come.

The real 'meat' of a syndication business is timeless material that needs little or no updating. My antiques articles were just the job.

First, the articles are 'unisex' – they appeal to male and female readers alike. Next, they were all illustrated, and as we know, pictures always help articles to sell. The third point is more subtle, but very significant as you'll see.

Collecting is fun, but it can be more than a hobby. A good collection, or a well-chosen individual piece of furniture, can prove to be a healthy investment. A hidden appeal of collecting, therefore, is the money factor. To underline this element I called the series of articles by the same name as one of my books on antiques: 'Collecting for Fun and Profit.' 'If you've got it, flaunt it' is good advice in syndication. You are presenting a lot of unsolicited material to the jaded eyes of editors. It pays to telegraph your message.

One final point about the collecting articles. The pictures were offered free, an appeal which may have topped all the others. I was able to do this thanks to a huge stock of photographs I had taken myself for earlier (already paid for) one-off articles on the various collecting topics. (It's important to make sure you get your prints returned soon after publication, or they'll disappear into a drawer and the editorial staff will hate you for making them hunt the thimble, at a later stage, when the article in question is long since filed and forgotten.)

When my pictorial stock ran out, I discovered that the major auction houses – Sotheby's, Christie's and Phillips – were happy to supply black-and-white shots for publicity, which means they see their business names in the captions. There is some anxiety here: editors don't always march to orders and the PR element may be missed off in the captions that appear in print. To help keep the press officer sweet and to maintain your own credibility, when you acquire complimentary illustrations from a press office, and send out the pictures with your article, write the captions yourself. Keep them brief, and make sure the brand name 'plug' is in there somewhere. Editors rarely bother to re-write something that is 'good enough'. Finally, send the press office cuttings from time to time, to show you are fulfilling your side of the unspoken bargain.

If the concealed money element in antiques articles enhances their selling appeal, you don't have to be Einstein to work out that articles on 'pure' money should sell like even hotter cakes. Now while I was working in the peripheries of financial journalism, writing on 'pop' topics – such as 'Get Rich Quick!', an exposé of money-making schemes for *What Finance* magazine, or 'If You Want to Look As If You're Made of Money', a *Daily Mail* piece on the jewellery we wear that incorporates coin of the realm, and suchlike – I had penned little on mainstream financial areas, like mortgages, tax, insurance, consumerism, and so on. But I knew a man who had.

Tony Hetherington, author of the 'Questions of Cash' column in the *Sunday Times*, had been syndicating his own work, in a small way, when I suggested I boost his marketing efforts via my own syndication agency. (Copywriter Lou de Swart suggested I call it 'Editor's Choice', but I extended it to 'Editor's Choice Features Service'.) I simply avoided Tony's own syndication territory and took in his articles on a sale or return basis, once an editor had requested a piece.

I 'sell' Tony like this in the publicity broadsheet that offers my syndicated articles:

SUNDAY TIMES COLUMNIST TONY HETHERINGTON WRITES OUR 'MONEY SENSE' ARTICLES

is the heading. The caption reads: 'Anthony Hetherington, columnist of the *Sunday Times* and contributor to Editor's Choice Features Service.' The spiel continues:

> Tony Hetherington makes easy sense of tax . . . personal finance . . . savings . . . investment . . . PAYE . . . pensions . . . mortgages . . . All the financial topics that baffle and worry your readers.

> He knows about money because he was trained by the Inland Revenue and rose to become a Senior Claims Examiner in charge of all tax refunds and the taxation of trust funds and settlements in a key central London area. As a financial journalist with television and local newspaper experience, he also knows about copy. He has that light, bright touch so rare among Fleet Street financial specialists.

The sale or return aspect is crucial, by the way. Of course, it makes sound business sense to take in stock on a sale or return basis. But it also helps sales to offer articles sale or return. This is no more than the literary world's version of the mail order come-on embodied in 'no obligation', 'send no money now', 'your money back guarantee' etc. Articles are usually ordered on the strength of the title alone, but the product itself is totally fugitive and may not suit the editor's particular publication for reasons of style or content. So you offer the return facility, but encourage the sale by inserting an inertia element, placing the onus of returning the solicited article firmly on the editor:

Ten Days' No Obligation Approval.
Any stock feature you ask to see is sent to you on 10 days' approval. Return it by the approval date stated [on your invoice] and you pay nothing. Otherwise, pay within one month from date of invoice, at the regular price.

As a guide to successful syndication subjects, look at this breakdown of articles I stock. It reflects fairly accurately the relative popularity of themes. I say 'fairly', since some titles have never sold, or only rarely. I'm an optimist who also knows the value of offering wide choice for its own sake.

Topic	Number of articles stocked
Collecting antiques	140
Money	66
Gardening	40
Business/motivational	35
Cookery	20
Start a business	18
Health, sex, sauce	14
Consumer	14
Ghosts, dreams, the occult	11

Also note ideas that failed. I offered a series of 10 unpublished articles called 'Starting Fishing'. Fishing is the UK's most popular 'sport'. I sold only a handful of fishing pieces. A cartoon series with a serious message (how to survive a hotel fire; car in the canal; heart attack; attack by an angry bull, mad dog, venomous snake, killer shark, mugger; nuclear disaster; flood; drowning) shared a similar fate.

Miffed by these home-made literary disasters, I floated a self-parodying series entitled 'Everything You Never Wanted to Know About . . . But Would Be Intrigued to Discover Anyway'. It offered inside information on why limp lettuce goes crisp when you put it in that special box in the fridge, how posh shoe-shop staff tie the laces on shoes so you never see the strands criss-crossing above the tongue, and so on. Do I need to tell you the fate of that whacky scheme?

How to price syndicated articles
Low is the short answer. Although editors know that syndicated pieces are the publishing equivalent of the Oxfam Shop, they seem to bite the bullet for all the reasons outlined above. But most of all because syndicated articles are *cheap*. You can sell almost anything on price, if the price is low enough. If you don't believe this, spend time going round car boot sales. Syndicated articles are also handy

for editors to have around in case a hoped-for story falls down at the last minute; if an advertiser takes space and creates new areas round the ad which need to be filled with copy, and so on.

To encourage casual sales, and to underscore the low cost of these articles, I always give editors a strong incentive to buy bulk. Thus my prices (1989 rates) are

1 title	£12
3 titles	£30
5 titles	£45
10 titles	£80

50 or more, by special negotiation. From only £250 for 50.

One client took three lots of 50 articles. It meant a lot of photo-copying and digging out of pictures, but it was a damned sight easier than creating £750 of original writing.

And my bargain-banging continues:

A Big 10 Per Cent Discount When You Pay With Order. The cost of our service is already low. But here is a way you can save money even on our low prices. Send payment with order and deduct 10 per cent from your bill (before VAT).

Since you save us money on our bookkeeping and accounting [by which I mean debt-collecting] we gladly pass that saving on to you. And you still have the same privilege of returning articles which do not please, within 10 days, for a fuss-free, full refund of your money.

Otherwise, pay within one month from date of invoice, at the regular price.

Secrets of syndication

How much should you pay other writers to syndicate their work? As little as possible. My richest uncle had the right idea. 'What is business,' he once said, 'but buying something for £1 and selling it for £2?' It follows that you are an even better businessman or woman if you can do the same deal with a raw material cost of 10p or 50p.

The cost of marketing a syndicated features service is fierce, pro-bably in the order of £1500-£2000 for a 500-address mailshot and another 500 printed leaflets in reserve for follow-ups. Besides which, the boss (me) has all the headaches, such as pulling in overdue cheques, handling queries, monitoring returns, and so on. You should indicate to would-be contributing authors that their input is the least of the operation. At the same time, it's worth saying that syndication can be a very lucrative way of marketing writing work and capitalising on research effort.

The research involved in any major article is as the base of the iceberg to the bit that sticks out above the surface of the ocean: you tend to do about seven times as much research as actually appears in print. Syndication work can draw on this otherwise wasted effort.

The mathematics of syndication are also cheering. A single Fleet Street 1000-word article might bring in between £120 and £250. My lowly 1000-word article on collecting cigarette cards sold to United Newspapers for £20 (to be syndicated via their own network), and about 20 or 30 times at an average fee of about £9. The research had been done for an article that was commissioned by *Art & Antiques Weekly*, and was paid at about £60. Better still, the syndicated article still has life in it!

The follow-ups I just mentioned are particularly important. My order form is part of the broadsheet that also contains the lists of articles to choose, thumbnail sketches of the authors, and so on. Once an order has been placed, the editor cannot easily re-order, having cut out the order form. So I always enclose a fresh broadsheet with every fulfilled order.

Why am I giving away all these secrets, you must be asking yourself. The simple reason is that Kogan Page, publishers of this book, are paying me to do so. Deep down, though, I don't fear competition. Partly because I'm that kind of a guy; partly because not many people ever amass enough saleable stock to make a go of syndication. But if you do, you will actually help my own syndication activities. You will encourage acceptance of syndicated work among editors. And that must help both of us long term.

How to syndicate a regular original column
The real plums in syndication are the regular slots; a column in a monthly, weekly, or even a daily paper. The daily, of course, is

likely to be a national, but not necessarily. Many cities have daily evening newspapers, while Scotland boasts three national papers, the *Daily Record*, the *Scotsman* and the *Glasgow Herald*, though these have poor coverage south of the border. In theory, you should have no trouble selling to these and to any number of other papers in different readership catchment areas.

You can do your own syndication, as I've shown above. Or you can try to get an existing syndication agency to handle your work. You don't get all the good stuff that comes back from successful syndication when you go out through a middle man, but you can benefit in other ways.

An agency with a name and a track record is taken seriously by editors, far more so than an unknown, writing in out of the blue with a flyer and a promise to deliver the goods, week in, week out. Deep down, the editor worries about the unknown loner, however brilliant his or her copy, whereas he knows that if a particular syndicated columnist can't hack it one time, the agency professionals will always produce cloned, ghosted copy, regardless, just to keep the paper sweet.

The longer you stay in this business, the more you will come to appreciate, probably with some dismay, that editors regularly favour the mediocre writer over the maestro, if the former makes life easier by being 100 per cent reliable. Reliability is a very rare virtue in writers. Why should this be?

Partly on account of the 'creative agony' involved; the best writing demands enormous concentration and energy. Partly because writing is, by and large, poorly paid, given the skills involved. So the writer may have to take on other work commitments to increase his income from writing, or suddenly spend more time doing the best-paying writing work. This is why it behoves us to sell our bespoke 'hand-made' product as shrewdly as possible and to make the most of mass marketing opportunities such as syndication.

How do you contact syndication agencies? In the UK, the leading journalist trade paper is the *UK Press Gazette*. The agencies, seeking business from editors who read the paper, take space in the classified advertising section. Other places to look are the *Writers' & Artists' Yearbook* and *BAIE News*, the journal of the British

Association of Industrial Editors. In America the most widely read journal going to newspaper and magazine editors is *Editor & Publisher*.

Now whether you decide to try your own thing or go out through an established agency, you need to know your market and the competition it presents. How do you do that? By studying what others offer, how much they charge, and how they present their wares. You may need to use some guile to achieve this.

Ideally, you want to see what the professionals offer exactly as they offer it to would-be editor clients. You are unlikely to achieve this writing in out of the blue as an unknown writer, which is where the guile comes in.

When you write to someone cold, all they know about you is contained on the piece of paper you send: your message and the credentials printed on the page. You work hard to send out the best possible query letter, why not give yourself a great entrée too, by building credentials that will help you achieve what you are trying to achieve? For the purposes of this exercise, why not become an editor?

I'm suggesting that you have some letterheads printed (at a cost of, say, £60 for 1000) which feature you as 'editor' of some concocted journal, the more general-sounding the title the better, as some syndicates specialise and won't care to send you material if your publication looks unlikely to use it. Is it worth all this trouble? The last time I surveyed the US syndication market there were 27 big syndication agencies in business. Wouldn't you like to see their publicity material? The bottom line, naturally, is how committed are you to winning.

Assuming you are game, try these fictitious magazine titles for size: *Out of This World, Tomorrow's Features, Riotous Read, Madelaine* – just be sure you are not duplicating an existing title of a publication! In the UK, at least, you can call yourself whatever you like, provided you do not do so for an illegal purpose. If it ever came to the crunch, and you were accused of being a fake, you could always talk about 'pilot issues' and testing the market.

And there's something else you should consider. Even the best of the mailing packs you'll receive from syndication agencies may not be as good as the best sales kits available to you from other sources. Listen to this. When my client the MI Group, the financial services giant, was on the point of launching as a new company, I discussed publicity material with Director of Operations, Peter George. George said he thought the bumf put out by other insurance companies was largely rubbish, but he was very impressed with the promotional literature produced by property companies, and this influenced MI thinking and arguably helped build its reputation.

Similarly with syndication. Yes, you should see what the market can offer, but you should also investigate the smart media packs available from the better quality magazine offices. A media pack goes to media buyers in advertising agencies. It contains all the information needed to convince the media buyer that the particular magazine is the ideal place in which to advertise the goods and services of the agency's clients.

The typical media pack contains sample issues, readership analysis, rate card (cost of advertising), technical details of ad and page sizes (known as mechanical data), readership surveys, and so on. The pack covers every angle and, most important, presents hard facts in a form that's easy to take and good to look at. Studying these you'll get a very good idea of what you need to include in your own syndication mailing. Consider the following:

- Samples of your column in a form that people can read. When I first started in syndication, I produced a leaflet which showed a number of published columns as paste-ups, reduced in size, and reproduced more as artwork

---

Figure 6. *Broadsheet (as big as* The Times*) publicity which promotes my own feature syndication service. Note the 'busyness' of the layout. And the large, clear order form with its 'tick' boxes. Make it easy for people to respond to your sales pitch and they will be happier to oblige. The photograph (top left) is itself an object lesson in journalism. At a British Association of Industrial Editors (BAIE) conference,* Daily Mail *photographer Monty Fresco explained how a photographer needed to be cheeky to get the best shots. I was. I needed a self-publicity shot that portrayed me as a photojournalist. I asked Monty to take my photo, using a roll of film I supplied, holding my newly acquired Leica. He could hardly say no. I used the shot also on my letterhead – and gave Monty a credit, as was only right and proper.*

than to be read. This is fine, as long as you also enclose readable examples of your articles.

- For the high-tech minded (and equipped) you might consider supplying examples of the column reproduced as bromides in varying column sizes, ready to be pasted up on the magazine's own standard page format (grid). The message here is that you are prepared to bend over backwards to make your work easy to use and cost-effective. You must also add that you can size the column up as the editor prefers. This degree of professionalism and helpfulness will not go unremarked.

- Enclose samples of illustrative material you can regularly and easily (which means cheaply) supply. This includes sketches, photographs, graphs, and so on. Much writing sells on the strength of the pictorial material supplied.

- Outline your own credentials for contributing the offered column. If you are long on expertise on your chosen topic and short on journalistic by-lines, go to town on your special knowledge and gloss over the writing bit.

- Enclose a 'head shot' (a self-portrait), preferably 10 × 8in and black and white, colour rarely being required. If that picture can 'tell the whole story', as press photographers are constantly being reminded their pictures should do, go for it. At a time when I was doing a lot of photographic work and trying to do more, I opted for a self-portrait of Mel Lewis as photographer, holding my new and much-treasured Leica M4-P. If a picture is worth 1000 words, what price a photograph of a man holding a camera?

- A covering letter. This is the 'hello' element of your pack. Like the verbal greeting, it should be brief – especially as you are hitting the reader with a stack of other things to consider. Outline the column and why you think the ed's readers will consider it a winner. Here's your chance to prove you really have studied the publication in question – if you can afford the time and cost luxury of targeting your copy precisely to the publication.

- Order form and sae. The form saves the editor having to write a letter. The less he has to do the better. Tick boxes are a great idea. Remember to restate your address and phone number on the coupon, as every good book on mail order advises. Why? Because people frequently lose the page from which they cut out the coupon, or the rest of the mailing, and could be left with a coupon with no address on that leaves them (and you) up a gum tree.

- I spend a lot of time slagging off designers. The best mailings are properly and professionally designed, not thrown together by a hack paste-up artist or counter clerk at an instant print shop. This doesn't mean you have to put up with designer tantrums: it's the design you want, not the designer. Find a good clear design on someone else's publicity that you like and which suits your purpose; then find a designer who's prepared to more or less copy it. The very fact that he (or she) agrees to this suggests you have already found a pearl among fey swine.

This type of direct mail marketing takes some pondering. It is an expensive exercise. Be sure you know what your total package has cost, including your own time, postage, stationery etc. Then keep a close watch on returns. Fortunately for us, syndication is also a peculiar type of mail order, where you don't know how much an order will be for: the editor can buy a single article for a few pounds, an entire run of articles, or commission you to contribute an original column that continues for years and earns you fortune and fame on top. Which reminds me. Always bang two drums with any syndication-getting blurb. My message goes like this:

Commissioned articles

The articles listed will be on your desk in just a few days. But if you have some special requirement, some favourite angle or topic you want covered, and it is not mentioned in these pages, let me know.

Cover every entrance – and exit

When you start you won't know where to put your greatest effort. Therefore, try every avenue. Advertise, mail out and proposition editors over the phone and in person. I suggest you do this via an initial phone call (which is covered in depth in Chapter 5), based on a well-structured sales pitch, though you must stay loose enough to react to anything the editor may suggest. The idea is to request a meeting, which you try to arrange over the phone, promising to send your mailing in the meantime.

The first phone call is 'cold'; you've sent in nothing. I suggest you then post your syndication pack so the editor has a couple of days, at most, to look through it. You are trying for two things here. You want him to have glanced at it and to be impressed. You don't want him to have studied it so hard he's had time to give it the thumbs down and then cancel your appointment. A personal presentation is much stronger and more vivid, and also aims to be the beginning of a relationship which leads to a long-running, preferably original, column. This is what long life, as a writer, is all about.

However, my personal view is that original columns are like gold dust and it is rarely worth a special trip to pitch for a column alone. I would always have a number of strong one-off feature ideas up my sleeve. Add that you have some ideas in that initial phone conversation. And be prepared to run through them quickly if asked to do so.

As for those exits . . . remember that nothing, including an ace relationship with an editor, or a regular column, lasts for ever. From time to time suggest ideas for new columns. Even if the editor ignores them he'll see that you're a live wire and admire you for it.

8
How to Get a Good Cash Collection Technique

One thing you should know, if you don't already, is that nobody actually wants to pay on time. In fact, people prefer to keep back money owed to you for precisely the reasons you want it paid. Securing prompt payment enables you to save on overdraft charges. Money idling away on deposit earns money from interest. And having cash in hand often enables you to secure better deals for anything you care to name, including the tools of your trade, such as a new word processor or office equipment, a new car or even a new home. Being sloppy about payment terms – yours – enables others to enjoy these privileges at your expense.

Besides these practical reasons for slowing up payment due to you, people will do it because that is the 'way of the world', human nature, whatever you wish to call it. Robert J Ringer, author of the outrageously successful American book *Winning Through Intimidation*, wised me up considerably to the metaphysics and psychology of slow and non-payment.

He said there are three main types of characters you will meet in business dealings. There is the chap who lets you know, early on in the game, that he is out to get as many of your chips as he can and you'd better watch out. Regarding writing, I suppose this equates to a client (or editor) who endeavours to pay as little as possible as late as he can get away with. This type, says Ringer, is at least honest. You know where you stand, and can be on your guard. Curiously, though, many people ignore even these clear warnings and go ahead and do business in an unguarded fashion, regardless. I talk later of the less obvious 'Indian signs' that spell pay-up trouble.

Then there is the businessman who assures you he has your best interests at heart, but still tries to chop off your fingers as you reach for your cheque. Finally, there is the businessman who does actually mean well, who has every intention of seeing you are treated fairly, promptly paid, and all the rest of it, but fails to live up to his own good intentions simply because, human nature being what it is, people cannot help putting Number One first, when it comes to the closing stages of a business transaction.

Now in fairness, Ringer was talking about his own line of work in real estate, which involved discovering marketable properties and finding and matching the property owners with suitable buyers, and taking a commission on the turn. Well, it seems to me the pay scenario may be somewhat different, but the personality types look awfully familiar.

Ringer also had a well-deserved crack at the success and get-rich-quick books, which promise untold riches, usually through some splendid sales system allied to gruelling hard work and the Zen-like practice of that most mysterious posture, a positive mental attitude.

The books failed to specify when success would come, stating only that 'ultimately' it must arrive. What they had overlooked, according to Ringer, was the single most important step in the sales litany, generally set down as a fail-safe system involving four steps:

1. Obtain a product to sell.
2. Locate a market for the product.
3. Implement a marketing method.
4. Close the sale.

Ringer insisted that the success books got people all fired up with enthusiasm, and possibly even equipped them to sell, sell sell; but that by far the most important, and arguably the hardest, step, getting paid, was simply missed out.

However, before we get started on actual cash collection technique, let's see how streetwise you are via a little quiz I devised for my writing students. They invariably score badly, and when one does get a right answer, I wonder how smart they'd be in a real-life situation. I'll tell you why later.

1. An editor says 'yes' to your article idea, or a company agrees to your PR proposals. What's the first thing you do?
2. In mid-assignment, your client – editor or company manager – alters the work specification, deadline etc. What do you do?
3. At what point do you send in an invoice for your work?
4. How long do you give the client to pay up?
5. What do you do when, because it's invariably not 'if', your client keeps you waiting for payment?
6. For one reason or another your client refuses to pay up. How long do you wait before taking him to court?
7. What's more important: a flow of cheques or a flow of work?

I'll handle this as though it were a Miss World contest and start at the bottom. If you answered 'work' to question 7 you're a ninny. Nothing this book shows you how to do is worth doing for nothing.

This is business – whether you're writing articles for an editor or promotional copy for a company. Getting work is often hard work. Writing well can be exhilarating, but it usually ends up being hard work. Getting paid regularly turns out to be not only hard work, but also depressing work. At the back of it all is the feeling that pay hassles are unjust. You've done your bit, why can't you have your 'end', the cheque that is rightly yours, in short order? Sadly, life is not like that. Let's face it, the only pure fun you're going to have as a writer is the 'cheque on your door-mat' part. And if you don't believe all this, try telling the gas man, the phone people, the mortgage company, or your partner that you're doing plenty of work: the only real problem is getting paid.

To *question 1*. Winning commissions is exciting. The great temptation is to show willing, impress with your professionalism and start work immediately. Resist it. Your first sensible step – indeed, your first professional step and also your first duty to your-self and your family – is to write a letter to the client outlining your 'understanding'. This should be brief, matter of fact and it should use everyday language:

Dear ...

I enjoyed our meeting of ... We agreed that I would write three 1000 word articles – 'How to Lose Friends and Infuriate People', 'The Great British Bottom' (a picture feature), and 'Hot Air Ballooning on a High Fibre Diet'.

You said the articles would appear, respectively, in the April, May and June 1989 issues of *Yours Sincerely*, and they would be paid at the rate of £100 per 1000 words commissioned. The Bottom piece will have a minimum of five 10 × 8in black-and-white prints to accompany the text, these to be paid at your usual rates, as used.

I'll bill you as the articles are submitted – you said you wanted them all on your desk by end February 1989 – with a 'pay by' date one month following the date of invoice.

With best wishes

Yours sincerely

MEL LEWIS

To be honest, I try to avoid including the deadline for delivery. Why give a sucker an even break? I've never been taken to court by an editor desperate for my long overdue work. But, by golly, have I had headaches and court cases involving money that is owed to me but is not forthcoming! As much as you are establishing your own case for payment, like any good lawyer, you are also keen to weaken your adversary's case wherever possible, because getting paid, like every other aspect of business, is all about winning, not entirely about being good or right.

The point about the pictures, by the way, and the use of the words 'as used', is to show that I don't expect to get paid for all the five prints I submit; just the ones that are chosen and appear in the magazine (fictional, as a matter of interest, like the titles).

When I say 'everyday language' I mean avoid making your letter sound legal and binding, like a contract. Never use the word 'contract', in fact; everybody, including people who are the nicest clients in the world, runs a mile when they hear that word. It's like the buzzer at the dentist telling you it's your turn next. It triggers a bad response, so avoid it. A contract sounds binding, restricting . . . *threatening*. The fact is, of course, that this 'understanding', this letter of 'agreement' *is* a contract and a legal document.

Your principal aim is exactly that: to establish good documentation. Look at documentation like the deeds to a house. Deeds give an owner 'good title' to a property. So with the letters you write confirming your assignments. They establish your right to (a) do the work and (b) get paid, should the matter ever come to court. The point is that a court action is *the last thing you want to happen*. It's time- and energy-consuming; it costs money, since time is money. And if you employ lawyers they cost money, too, big money. So you work backwards from that abyss.

Clients mainly give you a bad time on the payment front when they think they can get away with it; sometimes, of course, it's just an inefficient payment system that's to blame for tardy cheques.

Showing you are businesslike in your dealings is a talisman to your own good fortune: it will actually help you avoid being given a hard time, because clients who might otherwise be disposed to give you the runaround (and this is always tempting when clients may themselves be waiting for payment from their various sources) won't want to tangle with you!

Besides, the more corroborative documentation you can muster, quietly, efficiently and without appearing threatening, the more you are likely to get your cheque without going to court, but merely by saying you will if pushed. Nobody in their right heads goes to court knowing they haven't a leg to stand on, and clients are no exception to this rule.

Question 2. What do you do when your client alters the work specification? If the client changes the ground rules for an agreed piece of work, simply note the changes – in a letter. However, altered specifications are treacherous territory. If you are commissioned to write one press release and the client suddenly wants two based on the same facts, briefing meeting, research etc, shout 'Yipee!' and reach for the phone. You may not want to charge double the rate, but you will want to up your fee, get it agreed, and then confirm it in writing.

Similarly where an editor wants more words, more pictures, more articles. The real problem is where the client wants less work than previously agreed, or cancels a project altogether.

Less work is a tricky one. Generally, I tend to go along with the 'seigneur system' that prevails. The client is the boss, I am the menial; every so often I get reminded of my lowly place. Pet owners will know the feeling. The status quo needs to be restated and reinforced, if it is to be preserved. From time to time you have to kick the cat, just to check that the world is revolving the right way and no one has seriously questioned or upset the accepted order of things.

Kicking up a fuss may blight what remains of the commission and sour a working relationship that took time to build. So I tend to suffer in silence. But the rule remains: put the revised specifications in writing.

Because bosses are, psychologically speaking, 'bigger' than you they are also inclined to be bullies. They like to push people around and they are intrigued to see how far they can be pushed. It's only inhuman [correct] nature after all. In other words, having discovered that you don't raise hell when your fingers are stamped on, they might take to stamping on your feet or your face, just for fun, although fun might be clothed in corporate jargon. So that your commission is cancelled on account of 'budgetary considerations', a 'reorganisation of duties', or 'refocused' promotional strategy. 'Regrettably', naturally. But cancelled it is.

When, for one reason or another, this does happen, what do you do? I know what the books say and I talk to other professional writers to discover how they handle themselves in such situations; but in the end my own experience is what counts most. I'll take journalism first, authorship next and PR last.

Quite often, newspapers especially, but also some magazines, operate a 'kill fee' system. Quite simply, if an editor doesn't like a piece of writing as submitted, or prefers the piece to be handled by their latest, prettier protégé, or whatever, he reserves the right to cancel the commission and pay a lesser sum, known as a kill fee (or some similar euphemism).

Now the first point to note is that no editor has this right automatically. The curious, and little-known, fact is that what counts in these matters – and I'm talking endgame, legally, here – is the writer's own 'house rules'. Put simply, when you commission a job from someone, any kind of job, from anyone, you take on board *their* working practices, assuming these are not outrageously at variance with the norm for their type of business. This is why it pays you to establish very early on what your 'rules' are – when you want to be paid, and so on. Because technically speaking, what matters is when *you* want to be paid, not when an editor (or any client) wants to pay you. Not many people know that, and even those that do don't want to know it.

Getting back to kill fees, these are only operative and acceptable if you, as a freelance writer, want them to be. Unless an editor has spelt out his financial arrangements for writing off an unsuccessful piece, and you accept those terms, you don't have to accept them when they are thrown at you, out of the blue, later in the day.

You don't have to, but as I say, it may pay you to be flexible, because it mostly does in business. Where an assignment is barely started before it's nipped in the bud, I say fine, give me your kill fee and thank you very much. Where I have done the entire piece of work and submitted it in good faith, according to agreed specification, I may feel differently. This brings us back, neatly, to that old initial accepting/commissioning letter.

The more detail you pack in the better. An accurate plain-language report of the editor's stated requirements is what's needed. If you can demonstrate – to a magistrate, if necessary – that you have fulfilled your part of the bargain properly and professionally you will feel more confident about holding out for the full payment that is rightfully yours. One of the most soul-destroying occurrences in journalism especially (it does happen in other businesses, but less often and perhaps less dramatically) is where an editor commissions work and then disappears, either because he is sacked or moved to another department, and someone else takes his place. The new broom doesn't exactly have to sweep clean, but it has to be seen to be doing a lot of sweeping, and somehow my work always seems to be a victim of the dustpan.

This happened to me on a national paper. I had been contributing regular, highly paid and highly rated pieces on consumer topics. Moreover, I was on the point of being given a firm commission on a run of articles, with an agreed generous fee, comfortable expenses, and all the rest of it – very close to that state of grace which we writers call being retained. In a trice, that editor was ousted by younger (and rancorous) blood, and my hopes were dashed. I had one commission in hand. It wasn't finished, but I quickly pulled it together and handed it in, together with some other ideas I thought might appeal to the newcomer. I always fear the worst but act for the best; I suggest you do the same.

With great reluctance on the part of the newspaper management, the completed commissioned article was paid in full, though never used, naturally: the costly wastage on national newspapers is worth a book in itself. I also researched a couple of items for the slime who had slipped into the editor's chair. This was paid, but the work never blossomed into full-blown articles, and soon and predictably enough, I gave that section of the paper up as a bad job.

The moral of this story is, when the going gets tough, make sure you get away with as many chips as possible.

So much, on this point, for journalism. As for authorship, I have a right sorry little tale to tell. While working as a sub-editor for *The Times*, on its newly introduced weekend section, then called Preview, I managed to pick up a regular little slot writing about antique fairs and markets, one of my freelance specialisms, you may recall.

The market section came to include street markets, and in true photojournalist tradition, I was out and about on the weekends with both camera and notebook, since having a picture accompany the feature (which was paid by the column inch) virtually doubled my fee for the assignment.

Out of the blue came a phone call from one of our best-known book publishers. They'd seen the column. Would I be interested in collaborating with another writer who had come up with a bright idea for a guide to street markets? This other writer was keen but inexperienced and unknown. I was a known Fleet Street writer and a pro down to my follicles, so the book had to be a winner – or so the project was sold to me. I agreed to split the advance and royalties 50/50. A mistake, as you will read.

I worked like fury on that book. I quickly discovered that my 'co-author' was pretty clueless on most counts, including writing, spelling, typing and research. I took two weeks' holiday and spent them writing and revising this book. It wasn't good, but it was nearly done and in a workable state for a final draft when the bombshell came. According to our publisher's intelligence sources, not one, but *two* rival publishers were bringing out comparable books and they were further down the road to publication than we were. Our publisher wanted to abort the book and pay us each half of the agreed total advance, which was, as I remember £1500; so £750 each. To make matters worse, my co-author and I had commissioned and paid £300 for some drawings to illustrate our book, this being a familiar responsibility of authors, and a handy way for publishers to save on costs, so we were each £150 down on the proposed pay-out.

I didn't like this deal, but eventually we both decided to accept the cancellation of the contract. In retrospect, I did one thing right and one thing wrong. When I realised that my writing partner was a pain I said as much to the publisher's editor. I made it clear that I was having to do a good deal more work than my colleague, with the result that when the doomsday announcement came, I claimed, and won, the right to take a lion's share of the advance. I was lucky: according to my own lights, I should have put my misgivings in writing, to be sure of a satisfactory outcome. The co-author could have contested the lopsided pay-off and might have won the right to sustain the original 50/50 deal.

What I – what we both – did wrong was not to ask (if that's a strong enough word) for an additional payment to reflect what we might have earned overall from the book by the end of its putative active life. After all, the book was nearly finished, and presumably would have sold at least averagely well. We were penalised because our publisher wouldn't keep his word. But I was so depressed, so drained of adrenalin from my unsuccessful efforts, that I didn't have the heart to push my justifiable claim to the limits. Remember:

you only get tired when you're losing. Try not to let being whacked or disappointed get in the way of your getting paid. It's easier said than done, I know.

The PR volte-face is far fresher in my mind. I'm living it as I tap out this chapter. I lie awake at night penning imaginary, angry but lucid letters to the principals involved who decided, on a whim, to chop my contract in two, halving my earning expectation from that source for the coming year. What am I doing about it? Complaining, loud and long. Normally I recommend writing letters that are as short as possible, with the proviso that a letter should be as long as it needs to be to get your message across – just like a headline or the body copy of an ad.

The letter I sent is long, part of the 'shaping up for battle' process. I say in my letter that other people may have to read this 'important' letter. Only a moron will fail to see I'm talking about people in black gowns and tatty white wigs. My contractual rights are clear and strong. But taking a hard line, as I am, asking for full payment of the cancelled assignments, may lead to the entire contract being chopped. No matter. I watched as my original deal for the year was pared to the bone. A man has to make a stand some time.

Question 3. At what point do you send in an invoice for your work? This has to be an easy one to answer. Where difficulty is experienced, this invariably points to some deep-seated malaise or malfunction of the 'examinee'. When *should* you send an invoice for work done? If the answer isn't screamingly obvious, ask yourself this: when do you want to be paid? Never? Eventually? Or as quickly as possible?

Suddenly it all swims into focus... You send your bill in *together with your completed assignment.* Not only does this get the payment routine started soonest, but it also overcomes another frequently cited reason for non-payment of a bill; namely, that your bill never arrived. The editor can hardly say the work didn't arrive since, like every professional journalist should do, you phoned a couple of days after sending the work in to check that it had arrived.

By the way, never ask if the article was satisfactory. First, because nine times out of ten the editor hasn't given it a second glance or even an initial one: the secretary may still have your envelope unopened somewhere. But most important, because asking for praise, as this does, is inviting trouble. Most people tend to the negative. Ask for something nice and you're likely to receive something nasty for your trouble.

Remember, too, that deadlines are rarely honest and accurate. So the sooner you start asking for your money the better. The intelligent, experienced editor gives himself plenty of time to 'get round to' specific issues of his publication. Besides, he knows how unreliable writers are, so he gives his wordsmith 'suppliers' ample time to miss deadlines and still be on time for the real deadline, known only to himself and selected staff.

When I ask my writing students these questions, I regularly get some flak. Aren't I inviting trouble, being forward or aggressive about getting paid? Aren't I likely to put people off by being upfront about money? The answer is yes! It does upset some people. But only those I want to upset. The sooner they're upset the better. Because they're the ones who are most likely to give me a hard time some other time, probably when I've done the job, and they've come to see that the article 'wasn't really right for our readership'. Or they'd like to keep hold of the piece and will be happy to pay for it, 'on publication', a synonym for 'maybe one day', or, more likely, 'never'.

On to *question 4*: how long should you give your client to pay your bill? The broad answer is as long as is usual for most practitioners in your line of work. This happens to be writing, so far as we are concerned, but journalistic payment systems are traditionally more scrappy than in 'real' businesses, so you can expect newspapers and magazines to take longer than PR companies and mainline businesses, such as retailing and manufacture, mainly through the sloth, inefficiency and prima donna attitude of editors and publishers.

In fact, the point is even more subtle than that. Remember that it is the writer who decides when he wants to be paid, not the editor or client, however unimportant you may be made to feel in negotiations. Ideally, and without labouring the point, you can establish that you 'expect to be paid a month after handing in my work'. A month is an inoffensive period of time in most writing contexts. It doesn't take a month to pass, process, sign and despatch a cheque. But a period of grace is expected and companies have systems. The wise writer gets to know, and rarely bucks, the system.

The editor-elect of a new business magazine asked me to write a number of articles. He gave me a tight brief and we agreed a generous fee and worthwhile expenses. The editor told me, in so many words, that his new employers were looking after him very well indeed, with a package that included a handsome turbo-charged saloon car.

As these publishers were unknown to me, and the publication had yet to hit the newsstands, it seemed prudent to discover what type of payment delay might be expected. 'Do you know something,' my editor friend said, as he eased himself further into the mock Louis armchair in the plush hotel foyer, and took a fresh sip of his cocktail, 'we haven't yet worked out a payment system for contributors.'

The man was a friend of a friend and an experienced editor, but he never answered my query about payment. It seemed to me that the status of writer-contributors was so low he and his team had not even got round to dreaming up a convincing lie to cover our imponderable lot!

Curiously, and very unusually for editors, the very next day he sent me a confirming commissioning letter. In fact, everything that pertained to his requirements was there in fine print, and yes he did mention the £120 per 1000 words I would be getting and 'some allowance for expenses'. But as to when this money would arrive, there was some difficulty:

> You also asked about payment, and I told you honestly that a system to cope with contributors' accounts is not yet even in existence. All I can say is that I'll push things through as fast as I can; but I can't, at this stage, lay hand on heart and promise payment within the month you suggested. I hope you will trust me on this.

Well, this editor was not in charge of his own fate, as it turned out. Not long afterwards I heard that the magazine that had never opened was closing down, the editor hadn't been paid, and the magnificent car, which he might realistically have expected to hold on to as a 'hostage' against the dough he was owed, had gone in for a service and been seized by the publishers.

The point is, words like 'honestly', 'hand on heart' and 'trust me' should prompt a cold sweat in any writing pro, and I suggest you respond to this reflex. I did. I walked away from this tainted offer of work without writing a word.

Talking of trust, you sometimes meet a client who, reluctant to agree the working understanding you have reached or your terms in writing, will throw that word at you when you press the point, as you must – 'Why do you need a letter? Don't you trust me?'

What matters, from a business viewpoint, is not whether you trust a person or not, but whether you have that piece of paper as evidence or not. Ringer suggests a response along the following lines to the 'don't you trust me?' client. 'I do trust you,' you say. 'That's why I know you won't mind agreeing these points in a letter.' A trustworthy person cannot possibly object to this request, and I'm sure you won't, is what you are really punching home.

Having said that, editors are particularly bad at confirming anything in writing. Professional wordsmiths are often reluctant letter-writers; it feels like working for nothing. So I tend to write my own confirming letters where I expect resistance. In a court, a client would have a tough time arguing that yes, he had received your confirming letter, didn't agree the terms or commission as stated, but hadn't bothered to write back to say as much.

When a self-styled director of a property company approached me and asked me to report on the viability of turning a large commercial premises in a major North London thoroughfare into an antiques market, with the rental and overheads being shared among numerous dealers in antiques and crafts, I agreed. But only for payment by COD – cheque on delivery. For all the size of the mooted project, my client still looked like a one-man band, with a beer gut that suggested he was the last one who got short-changed in his deals.

The guy agreed, however. I researched and wrote the report and took it along to a rendezvous in his office. It was a good piece of work. Informed, thorough, readable. He thanked me, smiled and said he'd be in touch – if the project went ahead he'd hinted that I would be lucratively involved in the PR drive that would launch the new market.

Not as cool as a cucumber, I reminded my fat friend of our pay-up arrangement. He went into a little routine. He started faffing about with his papers, opening drawers, searching his pockets, the floor. It was like some human version of the frustrated water buffalo's displacement activity I'd read about in Desmond Morris or somewhere.

He was, he said, looking for his cheque book, which – surprise, surprise! – was nowhere to be found. I said I'd wait for him to find it. He said he'd send the cheque on, through the post. He said his secretary must have gone off with it. I said my time was my own and my diary undemanding that afternoon. Eventually, he found the book and I got my cheque.

Another time I wrote four pieces for a newsletter proprietor. A friend had warned that he was a stinker over payment. He was also a rich man with a disdainful manner. I named a high price and said I expected to be paid when I handed in the work. He smiled and agreed. I confirmed our understanding in writing, and went one step further. I included a carbon copy which I asked my new client to sign and return in the sae enclosed. He did, quickly.

And do you know what happened when I handed in the articles? You should do. You've heard it before. Mr Newsletter couldn't find his cheque book. He too went into that strange ritual I'd seen with Mr Antique Market and concluded that he hadn't brought it with him or the secretary had run away with it. I stood my ground, as before. And, lo and behold, the cheque book did appear as if by a miracle, and I was, albeit reluctantly, paid.

What would I have done if these two characters had stone-walled me all the way? Would I have left, unpaid? Would I have grabbed my work and flounced out of the office? I try not to think about it. What I do think about is that even getting your hands on a cheque doesn't mean you've been paid. Cheques can bounce and they can be cancelled. The fact that a cheque is a contract in law and gives immediate and just cause for court action is true, but baloney. Yes, you can sue. But that takes time, and time is money. And if the client really doesn't want to, or can't, pay, where does that leave you?

Well, I'll tell you. I once did some work for one of our seedier soft porn publishers. It was a mistake, and I'm ashamed of it, but it was an easy piece of work and times were hard. He didn't want to pay, even though the article had been published. I turned up at his equally seedy premises dressed in the sort of gear football hooligans seem to favour. Nothing especially vicious, just jeans and an old leather jacket, scruffy enough to relay the message that I wouldn't mind rolling on the floor or roughing up Mr Pornpublisher, should it come to that.

At his office I discovered a special automatic locking entry system operated by the magazine staff. Only those who were expected and welcome had a chance of getting in. Presumably they had a problem with flashers as well as writers who'd been given the runaround.

I got round this minor hurdle by dashing through the automatic gate in the slipstream of a visitor who had been cleared for entry to the inner sanctum. I found my wally of a publisher, gave him a right verbal dressing down in an embarrassingly public place, and walked out, cheque in hand. I should have got him to make it out to pay cash, but I forgot. I'm good; I'll leave it to you to become perfect.

But I did go straight to the bank branch, which happened to be local, and got the clerk to phone Mr P who agreed to let me take my money on the spot, in readies.

Question 5. What do you do when your client keeps you waiting for payment? This is not one of those things that happens from time to time. This is a fact of business life; it will happen almost as surely as the sun will rise tomorrow morning, the only imponderable being whether you or I will be here to see it.

Mind you, recently I had two clients who paid me ahead of time. I was very suspicious. Who were they trying to impress? When they failed to live up to their own record, second time around, I was even more worried than I would have been if they'd kept me dangling for payment in the time-honoured way – that's how cynical a writer can get!

One important point: what are you entitled to do when your bill goes unpaid? How quickly can you act? Assuming you have clearly established your payment terms (more of which at the end of this chapter) you are suffering from breach of contract from midnight on the day you said you wanted to be paid. Only a dolt would act on this fact, but it's as well to know where you stand legally.

What I do is this. I wait a couple of days, in case the cheque genuinely is where it is very often said to be, but rarely is – 'in the post'. Then I write on the bill a little note, apparently to myself, saying that this is the 'first reminder', plus the date. I photocopy the bill and send it. I do the same thing a week or so later if this pulls no response, scribbling on it 'second reminder', plus the date. Also a verbatim report of any phone conversation I may have had with an 'officer' of the company, relating to the debt.

Depending on a number of factors, such as how friendly I am with the editor, how familiar I may be with the payment clerk, how much money is involved, how much I am worried about non-payment with this particular company, how busy I am, and so on, I may phone to get a personal view of what problems there may be.

I choose my words carefully. I said to a recent slow payer: 'I'm having difficulty finding your cheque in the post.' It made light of a delicate situation, and also did the trick: the editor made some crack to his secretary about it being a trivial amount, and asked her to get the cheque sent out to me right away.

I also have a special red ink stamp that I had made up using special artwork. It doesn't so much say as scream off the page the words 'PAYMENT NOW DUE'.

I asked the designer to mimic the packing case style of typography. You see it on cases stamped with the words 'FRAGILE' or 'DANGER'. I may use this stamp to liven up these reminder invoices.

When it gets to number 3 in the series I start to worry, especially if there has been no telephone contact or where money has been promised but hasn't yet dropped on to my doormat.

I have another red stamp (both of these are Trodat Printy 4913 gadgets, available to order through many newsagents, by the way) which says 'RECORDED DELIVERY'.

RECORDED
DELIVERY

I use this only in dire straights. It's also useful with letters sent recorded delivery. The thinking behind this gadget and its imprint is simple, but largely unappreciated by the writing beginner. If you send out a letter by recorded delivery there is a yellow label on the envelope attesting this fact. When it arrives at its destination someone is supposed to sign it in, and that is your, and the Post Office's, proof of delivery. In practice, my own postman occasionally posts Recorded Delivery letters in my door when I am out, where clearly no one has signed anything in. Apparently, filling in the card obliging the would-be recipient to pick up the letter or parcel from the local sorting office (where the fact of receipt is noted in a book) is too much bother. I presume other Postmen Pats operate similar time-saving dodges.

Even where the letter is handed in at the client's office, perhaps to the Post Room, and delivery is actually recorded, it probably passes to a secretary who removes the envelope and sticks it in a bin, thereby destroying any sign that the letter was sent Recorded Delivery. The editor/publisher/client/accounts manager may never know that the reminder bill was recorded! Think it through. It's nuts, but it's true.

However, stamping the copy bill with a bright red 'RECORDED DELIVERY' stamp leaves the addressee in no doubt that this is a Mel-monitored missive that demands urgent consideration and, more to the point, action.

Question 6. How long do you wait before taking your client to court? I don't like taking clients to court, and I don't like courts. People wax lyrical about the so-called small claims court (actually the county court) which is supposed to be so easy it's almost fun to sue someone. The truth is, there are innumerable potential pitfalls, concerning such things as the court having to 'serve' the defendant at the registered office of the company, your having to decide which directors to sue, and so on and so forth. Don't tell me this is trivial, foolproof. I know better.

I asked my solicitor to sue a client who owed me £1000. The client lived in North London and I supplied the name and address of the client's company's registered office, also in that area. The work I'd done related to an event which was held in Dorset, though all the publicity work I'd done had been in my other home in Norfolk. I also operate from Islington, London. Where should this client be sued; in which court, in other words?

According to the rules, the court to use is either the one in the district in which the debtor lives or works, or the court in the area where the debt was incurred. I knew from experience that it pays to make it as hard as possible for a debtor even to appear in court.

I wrote some material for a publishing company in Southampton and insisted, successfully, that the contract was made in Islington, with the result that the action went to a court a few hundred yards from my office. The editor detested having to call all the way to London from the South Coast to answer the charges, but come he did. He tried to get the magistrate to switch proceedings to his local court – and failed.

I never saw him again. I won the next and final round. Mind you, I never got paid: my client went bust. But at least I'd caused him some anguish and put him to some expense.

For reasons which you will now understand, I was at pains to get this current case heard in a Norfolk court. After all, I'd clinched the deal in Norfolk, and I'd done most of the written work in Norfolk. And last, and by no means least, this client would find getting to Norfolk a pain in his turkey.

Guess what happened? My solicitor somehow let the pre-trial take place in Dorset. He appointed agents to be present at this hearing, and now expects me to pay for the privilege! When we have the next pre-trial, it will be at a court of my choosing. And I won't be paying my myopic legal eagle to perform. I'll do it myself. Now I'm refusing to pay his bill for the Dorset outing!

For all these reasons, and others too numerous to go into, you really should avoid court action where at all possible. Even having won a number of cases, I'm still a million miles from getting paid.

The bailiffs went in, but they came away empty-handed. It's so easy for a determined won't-payer to cry that all the saleable goods that could be taken away and auctioned to pay you belong to his wife, his mum, whatever. Or all the truly tasty stuff – TV sets, videos, cameras, cars – 'go for a walk' as soon as the client knows a visit from the bailiff is due.

There's something else as well. Bailiffs aren't paid by results, they're salaried. It's different in a High Court case. Instead of the Warrant of Execution that entitles the unmotivated bailiff to move in, here the Writ of Execution enables the Sheriff of the county to do his worst. Sheriffs have a much better track record. Know why? They work on a commission basis.

You will have gathered from the peculiar vehemence of this chapter and the astonishingly detailed inside knowledge concerning debt collection lore that the topic is an engrossing one. You bet! My life depends on it, and so may yours.

I've covered most of the important points, but not all. There is one other irritating question I like to ask my writing students.

What should you put at the top of the piece of paper you send to an editor, or a client, that tells them how much is due to you? Usually a hand shoots up: 'Invoice!' What's an invoice?' I snap back. This foxes the class. Eventually we arrive at the word 'bill'.

A bill, I explain, is an emotive and a motivating word. A bill prompts people to act, to reach for their cheque books, or it should. The word 'invoice' is no more than a label. An invoice is a piece of paper clients file and forget.

I press on. What do you want a client to do with your 'bill'? 'Pay it!' Now, you're getting somewhere, I tell them. So you could give your bill a little headline: 'BILL TO PAY.' It works. Try it.

And as I said earlier, all those clients who are upset by your 'forwardness' are exactly the ones you want out of the closet first. They're the ones whose cheque-signing fingers will cramp up quickest.

Finally, you must state your terms. I do it like this.

TERMS
E & OE

Cheque to be received by . . .
Cheque made out to Mel Lewis, please.

'E & OE' means Errors and Omissions Excepted. In other words, if you leave off a nought the client can't hold you to the incorrect lesser sum. The 'Cheque to be received by' date is more subtle than it looks. You don't want the cheque 'sent' or an account 'settled' by a particular date. You want the cheque in your hot hand, hence the word 'received'; it's unequivocal.

As for who the cheque should be made out to, it always drives me barmy, when I'm on the point of paying a bill, that the morons who sent it in make me search high and low to discover this elementary, yet crucial, piece of information. Don't be dumb, be paid.

Here are some more tips – and tricks – to help you get paid on time, every time.

Find out if your client has a preferred billing system. Don't worry about why they like it like they like it. Just give them what they want. Time and again, in my early days as a writer trying to earn a crust, I waited months to be paid, only to discover, long after my due date had well and truly gone by, that the firm only paid numbered invoices. From then on I always numbered invoices, where this is called for, with the first number that comes into my head, and a couple of letters attached, for good measure.

Always check out any idiosyncrasies of a billing system. One builder, about to work for a council, was told by other suppliers that getting paid was a bind and a half. This shrewd builder asked the council if there was a billing system they favoured. As it turned out, the council had an entire handbook on the subject. By following the rules in it, our builder not only got paid at an acceptable gait, but he also got stage payments – and all because he had asked the right questions at the right time.

As you probably know, clients pay their most powerful suppliers first. Not necessarily the biggest or the richest, but the ones they view as indispensable to their own business. Such suppliers enjoy a high profile as of right. However, it is possible to manufacture your own high profile. In fact, any small fry can do it.

What you do is phone the accounts department before the due

date on your bill. Say, a fortnight or ten days prior, this being the actual time it takes to raise, process and mail out a cheque. You ask, quietly, courteously, if they have received your bill to pay, if all is in order. Then get them to confirm that your bill will be paid on or before the date specified.

The best way of all to ensure prompt payment may be bribery and corruption. Find out who is the 'gaffer' in the bought ledger department, and take him or her out for a good, but not sensational, lunch. Then keep this VIP topped up with an after-work drink, bottle of single malt scotch at Christmas, and so on. Try it. You've nothing to lose except your legs.

9
How to Be and Stay Motivated

As I write, a major client has just cancelled half my contract in a cost-control exercise. Does this motivate me? You bet! No one cancelled half my mortgage, electricity or 'palimony' bill.

Will I get angry or will I get even? I decide to do both. The breach of contract is obviously actionable, but I'll try not to act through the courts, because solicitors are dumber, less motivated, and therefore slower than me. Yet they charge more for their time than I do. Such is the way of the world.

The anger will turn into aggression. I'll use it to win more assignments and better clients than the ingrates who have done me down. In the meantime, like anyone else in such circumstances, I also start to get morose. Life is hard, and then you die, what an unlucky devil I am, kind of thing. When suddenly, in the same week, I get two phone calls from prospective clients. You may have missed that one. They phoned me; I did nothing to solicit business from them. This is a turn-up for the books.

They'd simply read my previous book and rung the telephone number I had carefully planted. These could-be clients were complimentary and also businesslike. Meetings were arranged, money discussed.

Home and dry I am not. But the sky looks brighter already. Lots of things motivate me. Glancing at the contents I promised my publisher for this chapter I see the line, 'Editors are content to use less talented writers who deliver the goods on time . . . ' It's true. It's also fiercely motivating.

I lost a column I'd run for years to a writer whose one claim to writing's 'hall of fame' is that he wants to be a writer. Technique, style, wit, gusto – all else is lacking. I tell a lie. He must have a plausible line in chat. He's managed to convince a good number of people, including the editor of the magazine and his clients (he also does PR, he thinks), that he can do what he says he can do. I guess he's also reliable, which was my problem. I got too busy and too well paid, and everything else took a back seat to my big-paying client. It's a pitfall to avoid.

I ask myself: do I want to work for clients who don't know good work from bad? The reply is honest but depressing. The truth is, I care more about good cheques than discerning employers. Most of us do.

Glancing back at the chapter synopsis I wrote, angling for this book commission, I read: ' . . . writing by the yard also means earning cheques by the yard.'

What do I really care about? Owning two houses, two cars, three motorbikes? I've done those things, sometimes at the same time. What I really care about, care passionately about, is being prolific and being good.

I've had good models. Trevor Deaves, Chief Executive of the MI Group, a client and a multi-millionaire in his early thirties, says chasing money is a mistake; it will run away from you. Be good at what you do, brilliant at what you do, and success/money will chase you.

Do I enjoy writing? In full flight, yes. It's exhilarating. Mostly, I enjoy 'having written'. I don't mean it's like banging your head against the wall, lovely when you stop. But working on the last draft, word-processing it to perfection, printing out the final version, mailing it off to the editor and seeing my work in print – that's what I call fun.

Similarly with publicity work. Mailings go out by the sackload. And then the phone rings. It's *The Times*, or the *London Evening Standard*. Tell me more about . . . Can you work up this or that particular angle? It's all wanted now, and usually it really is now or never with journalists. This is exciting. I also suspect it's at this point that many PR people fall flat. If they haven't worked in newspaper offices, if they don't know how to dig up information in minutes and work it up into usable text in typing time, they will miss the deadline, or the editor's enthusiasm for the story wanes.

I've read countless books on writing technique and assimilated all the authors' tips on getting and keeping those creative juices flowing. So should you. Read everything. See what works for you. And discard the rest. Five tips do, however, stand head and shoulders above the rest:

1. Do it now. I find that a very motivating slogan. There's a corollary. If you do it, it's done. It sounds wet, but it isn't. There's a certain brutal, childlike honesty to it. Perhaps this is what Zen is all about.

In this writer's world it translates into something very positive. I get up, throw on a dressing gown and start writing, or revising yesterday's efforts. I try to do this unwashed, unshaven, unbreakfasted. You know yourself how easy it is to soak that little bit longer in the bath, how easy it is to linger over the toast and treat yourself to another slice, read the post or the papers. I turn exercise into a reward for getting on with the job. Breakfast is a reward for doing the exercise.

Sometimes I get carried away and the wash part, the least important bit if you think about it for ten seconds, gets left till teatime or later. Who cares? What matters is . . . nothing comes between you and your work and the work gets done.

2. Leave something undone. This was Somerset Maugham's idea, I think. He suggested clocking off work in mid-sentence. The idea being that you will at least know how to end the sentence when you return to your desk, and that once the keys are being hammered you won't be able to stop – at least that's the theory. I find this works, and also a more general adaptation of the principle.

I study research material at the close of a day's work, or read a draft which needs to be revamped, and then put it down and mentally 'clock off'. The next day I know exactly where I'm going. The 'parabrain' has been hard at work, according to the latest theory.

3. Start anywhere. At school we were always taught the importance of planning, of structuring our essays. In the real world of professional writing I suggest you try a more anarchic approach.

Start where you like – or more precisely, where you can. Do whatever's easy, but do something and do it now. This doesn't mean you haven't thought about what you are going to write. You have. You've rooted about in your cuttings file or the library and brainstormed yourself half to death. What you haven't done is formalise your thoughts.

It's very simple. If you know what you're going to include, it doesn't matter at what point you write that paragraph or sentence. Ordering writing, 'stitching' it together so the joins don't show, is a doddle compared with actually constructing the stuff. Talking of which, I prefer the table-top, scissors-and-paste method of construction. It's low-tech but very tactile. And it works.

4. If you can't write it here, write it there. Translated, this says that when you get bored with your typewriter or keyboard you should remove yourself to the pub or the park and carry on working. The change of environment is refreshing and energising. At a pinch you can also switch to some relevant subsidiary activity, such as research or revision.

5. Find a level of 'tech' that turns you on. I was very happy with an Adler Gabriele 35 for many years, arguably the finest mid-weight portable ever built. I had a pink IBM executive and, later, a number of electronic typewriters, with and without memories.

Having spent a lot of time writing about high-tech equipment (you don't need to use it to do this), I decided the time was right to take the plunge. I couldn't get my Amstrad to work at all at first and retired defeated, at least for a while.

I later invested in a bargain-priced NEC Starlet flip-top portable, which did wonders for my productivity – and my image – as I travelled between my London and Norfolk homes by train. The gadget conked out dramatically more or less on the day the three-month guarantee expired.

I now work with a black plastic technomiracle the size of two paperbacks, called the Sinclair Z88. It's my third in seven months and all under guarantee. Do you need to know more?

I see it like this. In spite of the razzamatazz (and I'm one of the copywriters guilty of generating this silly optimism) we are in a very elementary stage with high-tech hardware. It's a headache and occasionally, such as when the machine decides to lose its (ie, your) memory, a nightmare.

But like Adam with Eve's apple, having tasted it, you won't be able to do without it. The answer is to 'trust in God and keep your powder dry'. The Sinclair has a tiny memory and I have a tiny amount of patience. So I do a lot of printing and keep relatively sane. Find what works for you and stick with it.

When all's said and done . . .

My writing students often ask simple questions. Such as: 'Can you earn a good living as a feature/commercial writer?' What is a good living? The national average as I write this book is about £12,000 a year. Fleet Street staff journalists don't earn less than about £20,000. I say it's possible to earn three 'average' livings doing what I've shown you in these pages. Is that a good living?

Our type of writing is exciting much of the time and gruelling hard work as well. Quite often I throw away the clock and pick up the drink bottle to get things done. Sometimes the effort leads into what feels like heart attack territory and I wonder if it's all worth the effort.

What is worthwhile is being able (sometimes) to call your time your own. Novelist-critic Anthony Burgess said that in the year he thought would be his last he wrote six novels. It's easy, he maintains. You simply 'write 2000 words before breakfast, and then you can call the rest of the day your own'. Easier said than done? The spirit of his message is spot on, and applies equally to commercial writing.

Being independent doesn't mean you can stop being nice to people you may not like or respect, but it does mean you can choose your bosses in a way that you cannot in a PAYE job. And if you spread your efforts intelligently enough you can walk away from clients who aren't up to your demanding standards and still earn a good living – or several.

Ultimately it pays a writer to become totally independent. This means owning the product, the means of marketing it and the profit. Such is the case with features syndication, but it could equally mean publishing your own newsletter, magazine, book, information leaflets, and so on.

You cannot imagine the pleasure and relief there is, having written a piece of self-publicity and realising that no one needs to be chased for copy approval, timing or cost controls. One client gives me a bad time even about grammar; being master of your own semi-colons is bliss and a worthy ambition in itself!

Being prolific is a must: exhilarating in itself and essential to keep the cheques covering the doormat. If you can't come to terms with computers, which will boost your output no end – I heard a middle-aged historian say on TV how threatened he feels by them – then find someone, possibly younger, who can. Use their services and get them to teach you the ropes.

Becoming successful gives you the licence and also the freedom to become more successful. Learn how to write by talking. Make brief notes, as if you were giving a speech. Put them in order. Know what you want to say – practise out loud. Then talk into a tape recorder and get someone to type up your copy. This apparent luxury can quadruple your output and then becomes vividly cost-effective, in spite of the secretary's fee. It's easy – once you get over your initial 'stage fright'.

The main bar to being prolific is nerves. Use every success to make a brave step forward. When an editor says 'yes' to your suggestions, when a fat cheque comes bouncing in, use that adrenalin to boost your confidence. Get to the keyboard and write something you've been agonising over and 'working your way round to'.

Learn how to write first and ask questions later. Revising copy is pure pleasure compared with getting started. And when you get good enough, though your first thoughts may not be your best, they will be *good enough*. And a writer can make a good living by being reliable and consistently good enough.

10
Useful Addresses

British Association of Industrial Editors (BAIE),
3 Locks Yard, High Street, Sevenoaks, Kent TN13 1LT;
0732 459331

British Rate and Data (BRAD),
Maclean Hunter House, Chalk Lane, Cockfosters,
Barnet, Hertfordshire EN4 0BU; 01-441 6644

Contributor's Bulletin (publishers of *Freelance Market News*),
5-9 Bexley Square, Salford, Manchester M3 6DB;
061-832 5079

Institute of Public Relations,
Gate House, 1 St John's Square, London EC1M 4DH; 01-253 5151

National Council for the Training of Journalists,
Carlton House, Hemnall Street, Epping, Essex CM16 4NL;
0378 72395

National Exhibitors Association,
29a Market Square, Biggleswade, Bedfordshire SG18 8AQ;
0767 316255

National Union of Journalists,
Acorn House, 314 Gray's Inn Road, London WC1X 8DP;
01-278 7916

Public Relations Consultants Association,
Premier House, 10 Greycoat Place, London SW1P 1SB;
01-222 8866

Society of Authors,
84 Drayton Gardens, London SW10 9SB; 01-373 6642

Press cuttings bureaux

Durrants Press Cuttings,
103 Whitecross Street, London EC1Y 8QT; 01-588 3671

Romeike & Curtice,
Hale House, 290-296 Green Lanes, London N13 5TP;
01-882 0155

Press release distribution and media targeting agency

PNA,
13-19 Curtain Road, London EC2A 3LT; 01-377 2521

Syndication and features agency

Editor's Choice Features Service,
Red Brick Cottage, 17a Broad Street, Harleston,
Norfolk IP20 9AZ

11
Further Reading from Kogan Page

The Business Guide to Effective Writing, J A Fletcher and
 D F Gowing

The Business Writing Workbook, Ian Stewart

Effective Presentation Skills, Steve Mandel

Going Freelance, 2nd edn, Godfrey Golzen

How to Promote Your Own Business, Jim Dudley

Improving Your Presentation Skills, Michael Stevens

Readymade Business Letters, Jim Dening

*Working For Yourself: The Daily Telegraph Guide to Self-
 Employment*, 10th edn, Godfrey Golzen

Writing for a Living, 2nd edn, Ian Linton

Index